A Mason's Work

A Mason's Work:

Reclaiming Operative Fraternalism Through Symbolic Self-Development

Brian Mattocks

A Mason's Work Press

2026

Dedication

For my family who believed in me before I did, and for my brethren in the craft for the same reason.

Author's note on the use of AI in this book:

It is tempting for an artist of any kind, to want to explain the manner in which the hand holds the brush, or the length of time it takes to arrive at just the right shade of rose to blush the cheek; as if the time and effort in many ways add value to the expression itself. It does not. It adds, perhaps, to the appreciation of the expression, but not meaningfully to the work. The expression must, therefore, stand alone; the painting is not sold with the brush used to create it, nor the paint remaining on the palette. What remains of the process must be inferred through texture and artifacts of the making. This gets much more difficult with large language models (LLMs), although there are certainly signs.

We live in a time when the tools we use in everyday life are evolving at a rate that is unprecedented. Oddly enough, this bleeding edge technological advance has led to age old common laments that "art is dead" and the "cheapening" of creativity. Similar remarks can be found in Victor Hugo's *The Hunchback of Notre Dame* regarding the death of architecture as a medium of expression and storage of history when faced with the advent of the printing press. I'll leave it to the reader to judge the validity of that argument.

What I call my knowledge is itself a copy of a copy of an interpretation of a cave painting made by someone who thought to share. This book itself is a cave painting of sorts, informed by a magical calculator, and all the paintings that came before, and as such no more nor less my own. What I can offer in terms of comfort, for those of you still struggling with the uncanny valley of co-creation using these types of tools, is that future generations will not stigmatize this in the same way we don't criticize the modern author who does not hand copy his texts for publication.

As tool use goes, the LLMs that I used are no different in this case than a hammer in the hands of a carpenter or stonemason.

Used appropriately and in context the hammer works at the will
of the wielder. The very nature of the tool itself requires the will
to power it, the technique to guide it, and the design to inform
its application. Discomfort with unfamiliar tools is not unusual,
particularly when those tools are new. Still, the ideas explored
here are concerned less with their means of assembly than with
what they ask of the reader. If this book is to be set aside, it is
worth being clear about the reason.

With warm compassion and care,
Brian Mattocks
Winter 2026 ~ Philadelphia

The Work & How to Use It

Freemasonry is a progressive science that has largely stopped progressing. While we have preserved the architecture of the lodge, we have lost the operative method of the craftsman; ritual has become a performance to observe rather than a tool to use. This work is a manual for the intentional refinement of consciousness, providing the scaffolding modern life no longer supplies. It offers a structured system the *Operative Protocol* for translating symbolic instruction into lived conduct and can be further enhanced with the resources available on our readers only webpage http://amasonswork.com/amwbookreader/

This book is structured to serve two purposes: it establishes why this approach matters (Parts One and Two) and provides the how of putting it into practice (Parts Three, Four, and Five).

For the Practitioner: If you are here for the practice, skip directly to Part Three to begin working with the protocol. The system functions whether or not you understand the developmental psychology behind it.

For the Scholar: If you need to trust the architecture before you build, start at Part One to understand the integration of developmental psychology, integral theory, and classical freemasonry.

For Reference: Part Five provides a comprehensive symbol reference using a three-lens framework to deepen your understanding of each instrument.

The perspective presented here is a functional lens for personal inquiry. It doesn't matter where you start. It only matters that you start.

Contents

PART ONE: A Mason's Work

The Architecture of Purpose

Across history, individuals have described an inner sense that
life is oriented toward a purpose not yet fully known. Damon
(2008) identifies this as a persistent desire for meaningful
direction that emerges long before a man possesses the
capacities to act on them. Whether viewed as a central
organizing force (Emmons, 1999), an anchor for identity in
suffering (Frankl, 2006), or an unfolding narrative (McAdams,
2006), this drive for purpose is the bedrock of the human
experience.

This search for the proper function of a man is the golden
thread of the Western and Eastern traditions. Whether
expressed through Aristotle's pursuit of flourishing or Paul's
vision of discipleship, both define the human project as a
deliberate reshaping of character to meet a higher purpose.
From the Stoic's alignment with rational nature to the
Confucian *Junzi's* deliberate cultivation, from the stabilizing
moral presence of the Talmudic *Tzaddik* to the Bodhisattva's life
of service, the conclusion remains the same: a coherent life is a
product of intention, not accident.

Freemasonry is the direct inheritor of this formative lineage. Where operative masonry once shaped apprentices through craft discipline and shared labor, speculative masonry preserved that architecture to shape thought, conscience, and character. Its degrees form a symbolic curriculum that guides a man toward maturity. It does not dictate his destiny; rather, it provides the environment where that destiny can be clarified through reflection, feedback, and progressive responsibility.

The Erosion of Scaffolding

For much of Western history, this maturation occurred within social structures that provided the necessary tension for growth. Identity emerges most reliably in environments that combine expectation, intergenerational interaction, and clearly defined roles (Bronfenbrenner, 1979; Lerner, 2002). Families, religious communities, and civic guilds once supplied the scaffolding required to cultivate self-regulation and a coherent sense of place.

Over the last century, these mechanisms of formation have collapsed. The decline of civic and religious participation has removed the traditional floor of developmental stability (Putnam, 2000). While digital connectivity has increased, meaningful relational contact has plummeted, leaving individuals in a state of isolated hyper-communication that offers no depth (Twenge, 2017; Cacioppo, 2008).

In the vacuum left by these vanished structures, predatory cultural currents have emerged. We see the rise of performative consumerism, where identity is a visible aesthetic signaled through products rather than an internal transformation (Bauman, 2000; Illouz, 2019). We see a culture of extreme productivity, where growth is equated with output and exhaustion is mistaken for commitment (Gregg, 2018). Finally, we see algorithmic mentorship, where recommendation systems prioritize emotional provocation over the slow work of discernment (Zuboff, 2019).

In one, growth is stylized. In another, it is brutalized. In the third, it is suffocated.

The modern candidate arrives at the lodge door with potential but without preparation. He feels the pull of meaning but lacks the tools to translate it into direction. Freemasonry can no longer assume the foundations it once received from the surrounding culture. It must now provide the scaffolding it used to inherit. The lodge must move from a place that *discusses* growth to a place that *produces* it through deliberate practices of reflection, dialogue, and shared accountability.

From Metaphor to Method

When Freemasonry transitioned from an operative guild to a speculative fraternity, it kept the symbols but lost the developmental method. The tools became metaphors, and the relationship between action and thought became a one-way street. To reclaim our operative identity, we must move beyond mere interpretation and establish structured practices that link symbolism back to lived experience.

This approach aligns with teleological behavior theory, which asserts that intentional action is what truly shapes character (May, 1953). By organizing the craft's symbols into a developmental framework, *A Mason's Work* provides the bridge from mental exercise back to operative execution. While these symbols are often viewed as static decorations, the work ahead will demonstrate how they function as psychological tools designed to shape perception and behavior in real-time.

Fraternal Care as Infrastructure

The lodge possesses the rare potential to serve as secular pastoral infrastructure. It is intergenerational, oriented toward moral discourse, and utilizes a shared symbolic language to externalize a man's internal questions. Its officers embody psychological roles, guidance, support, and mediation, that provide a liminal space for genuine transformation (Turner, 1969; Bell, 1992).

This is not therapy; it is a relational context. By encountering the same brothers across years, a man's insights are allowed to accumulate and integrate. This integration of symbolic instruction with communal care creates a rare *cognitive toolkit* for life. It provides a framework for examining motives and aligning actions with values. In a landscape of fragmentation, the lodge offers a stable environment where a man can finally see himself clearly.

The Architecture of the Journey

The developmental logic of this work is informed by an integral understanding of human growth. Drawing on the work of Ken Wilber (2000), we recognize that development is not a flat progression but a recursive unfolding through levels of increasing complexity and consciousness. This framework ensures that symbolic instruction remains attuned to the diverse levels of being present within a lodge, allowing the craft to speak to a man wherever he stands in his own maturation.

This is supplemented by the principles of Formal Axiology (Hartman, 1967), which provides a lens for understanding how we value the world. By distinguishing between systemic, extrinsic, and intrinsic value, we can better assess how Masonic decisions align with moral principles rather than mere practical necessity or structural convenience. Underpinning the entire architecture is the premise of the tools and symbols as instruments.

An instrument differs from a metaphor in its use. Metaphors invite interpretation; instruments enable operation. When symbols are treated as metaphors, their function is discretionary. When treated as instruments, they exert constraint and shape conduct regardless of a man's current mood or interpretation.

From a cognitive perspective, these tools work by offloading regulatory demands from working memory into external structure (Norman, 1993). By providing a concrete reference point, they reduce the mental load required to monitor behavior.

They function as amplifiers of internal feedback. Within the lodge, this operative use is reinforced through ritual repetition, gradually transforming an external instrument into an internal capacity.

The Integrated Call to Fraternal Action

Possessing the tools of development is not the same as enacting them. The contemporary lodge faces an adaptive challenge: it can remain a ceremonial social club, or it can reclaim its role as an institution that shapes men of integrity (Heifetz, 1994). To become a system that supports such development, the craft must adopt deliberate practices with intention.

We live in an era where the traditional social scaffolding has collapsed, leaving the modern candidate with potential but without preparation. In this vacuum, the lodge must move from a place that discusses growth to a place that produces it. This work is not an attempt to invent a new freemasonry, but to provide a functional protocol for the one we have inherited, moving from a common understanding of what the tools mean to a disciplined practice of what the tools do.

True development is relational. We progress toward a more complex identity only when we participate in communities that balance support with challenge (Kegan, 1994). This requires a shift from a passive to an active conception of membership.

- **The Rituals** are not performances; they are invitations to reflect on conduct, motive, and consequence.
- **The Symbols** are not artifacts; they are instruments that shape perception and decision-making.
- **The Offices** are not titles of status; they represent the psychological and relational functions necessary for the health of any community.

This is not a nostalgic plea for the past, but a realistic response to the needs of the present. In a culture of performative identity and algorithmic noise, men require a center of moral

and civic formation. The relevance of the craft will not be
secured through public relations, but through its ability to form
individuals who live with clarity, integrity, and compassion. The
tools are available. The structure is intact. What is required
now is the commitment to the work; the realization that the
success of the craft is ultimately found in the life of the engaged
freemason.

PART TWO: Masonic Symbolism Applied

Symbols as Instruments of Development

Symbolic systems are not ornamental; they are mechanisms for structuring attention and coordinating behavior. Across history, religious traditions and craft guilds relied on shared symbolic vocabularies to orient members toward common standards of judgment. These symbols act as condensations of meaning (Turner, 1969) that embed values within lived practice (Geertz, 1973). They do not merely communicate ideas; they regulate behavior.

Freemasonry stands within this lineage. Its working tools, the square, compasses, level, plumb, and gauge, encode principles of proportion, integrity, and discipline. Originally designed to produce sound physical structures, their speculative function guides the formation of thought and conduct toward a similar reliability.

This logic is operationalized through the functional layout of the working group, where the Role (Office) establishes the necessary authority to move the labor forward. Within this structure, the degrees (Apprentice, Fellowcraft, and Master) function as implements, symbolic aprons, that the Role applies to define the maturity, scope, and responsibility of the current task. By viewing the degree-state as an implement rather than a destination, the Mason treats developmental milestones as tools used in the role to navigate the path from potential to refinement. However, this function is only operative when engaged deliberately.

The unique value of the lodge is *protective abstraction*. A common symbolic language allows men to examine personal questions without the psychological framing or personal exposure that often triggers defensiveness. One can speak of being out of level or beyond the compasses without the weight of a private confession. By lifting experience into a shared frame, the craft enables care without exposure and correction without accusation.

Prerequisites for Symbolic Work

A tool only functions if the worker can perceive his own action as it unfolds. Developmental systems presuppose a level of self-regulatory awareness that is rarely cultivated in modern life (Posner & Rothbart, 2007). Without the capacity to monitor internal signals, effort, strain, and emotional pressure, regulation remains external. A man may achieve a goal, but his development remains dependent on structure rather than perception.

Masonic tools address this gap by orienting attention *before* prescribing intention. They make the implicit visible. The square directs awareness to the alignment of action; the compasses to the boundaries of desire; the gauge to the use of time. In this sequence, attention precedes regulation, regulation precedes intention, and intention becomes an act of clarity rather than a reaction to external enforcement.

From Action to Awareness

Developmental systems succeed when they follow a specific

sequence: awareness of action, then awareness of internal signals, and finally, interpretation. Behavior is the most stable entry point because it is concrete and verifiable (Kolb, 1984). By anchoring reflection in what has actually occurred, we avoid the trap of narrative reflection where a man generates explanations for his behavior without gaining the capacity to change it.

This capacity to notice internal signals in real-time is *interoceptive literacy.* These signals provide the feedback necessary to know if an action is proportionate or misaligned. When this literacy is high, regulation occurs in real-time. When it is absent, regulation must be imposed by rules or consequences (Baumeister & Vohs, 2007).

Freemasonry cultivates this literacy indirectly. The compasses do not ask for an analysis of desire; they constrain it, making the internal *sensation of excess* perceptible. The gauge does not lecture on time management; it structures effort so that *resistance and urgency* can be observed. This external scaffolding facilitates internal awareness more effectively than direct introspection (Vygotsky, 1978).

To make this more direct *A Mason's Work* uses an ARAA sequence, a reflective cycle designed to move the Mason from abstract symbol to concrete conduct:

- **Awareness:** The initial encounter with a principle or the surfacing of a hidden challenge.

- **Reflection:** The inward examination of one's current relationship to that principle.

- **Analysis:** The discernment of choices and their long-term consequences.

- **Action:** The manifestation of insight through disciplined behavior.

This sequence mirrors the internal processes required for genuine moral formation. Symbols are not static images; they are psychological tools that only gain power when they shape perception. Within the lodge, reflection gains depth when it is shared, and intention gains stability when it is anchored by accountability. While psychological tools support this work, they remain strictly operative in nature. A gauge does not measure time for the worker, and a trowel binds nothing unless the hand applies it. The value is found not in the system, but in the application.

The Functional Definition of the Operative

A potential point of friction for the modern reader is the term operative itself. Historically, this referred to the physical labor of the stone mason's trade. In the context of this work, however, returning to the operative does not imply a literal return to the quarry. Instead, it describes the *functional application* of speculative knowledge.

To work operatively is to move from metaphor (the tool as a symbol of a virtue) to method (the tool as a mechanism for change). While speculative masonry preserved the architecture of the craft, the *Operative Protocol* provides the means to inhabit it. This is the transition from observing the ritual to executing the protocol on the stone of one's own daily conduct and character.

- **The Stone**: This is the unprocessed, often messy experience of your daily life.

- **The Labor**: This is the application of symbolic constraints to that experience to move from unexamined habit to a purposeful life.

- **The Result**: This is not a finished building, but a refined man who is fit, reliable, and capable of supporting those around him.

By viewing the operative as a cognitive and behavioral discipline, we fulfill the craft's original intent: to serve as a workshop of self-development. The tools are applied to the mind and the will, ensuring that the Grand Architect's design is manifest in the life of the freemason.

PART THREE: Working with the tools

The Shift: From the Quarry to the Workshop

In Part Five, we inventory the toolbox of the craft, defining the roles, implements, and systems available to the freemason. However, a toolbox sitting in the corner of a room performs no labor. The *Operative Protocol* is the act of picking up those tools and approaching the stone; the unprocessed, often messy experience of daily life.

A benefit of this protocol is *Protective Abstraction*. By lifting a personal conflict out of your immediate emotional field and placing it within the symbolic architecture of the lodge, you create the distance necessary for objective work. You move from being angry or confused to using the level or the square to measure it.

The Operative Protocol

The symbolic system is not a collection of definitions to be memorized; it is a set of instruments to be applied. This protocol provides a structured way to move from a state of reactive unprocessed experience to a state of ordered growth.

When you encounter a challenge, whether it is a conflict at work, an internal feeling of depletion, or a complex decision, do not rush to the symbols. Follow the sequence of the craft. We begin with the environment, establish authority, and only then reach for the tools.

Step 0: Interoceptive Awareness (The Knock)

Before the protocol begins, there must be a signal. This is the knock at the door a physical sensation of tension, urgency, or misalignment.

- When distressed, it's difficult to separate all of the different thoughts, feelings, and physical sensations you may be experiencing. Taking a moment and a few deep breaths to take inventory of what you are experiencing strengthens awareness and enhances future work.

- **The Work:** Identify the internal signal (e.g., a tightening in the chest or racing thoughts).

- **Narrative Tissue:** We do not ignore these signals; we use them as the Tyler's alert that work is required.

Step 1: Entering the Work (Spaces)

Some situations are difficult not because they are complex, but because they are approached in the wrong space. Spaces describe the environments that permit different kinds of effort. By naming the space first, you prevent your ego from moving straight into defense or premature action.

The Practice:

1. **Name the Situation:** Write a factual, one-sentence description. (e.g., I feel resentful about the amount of overtime I am working.)

2. **Select the Container:** Ask where this work belongs:
   - **The Lodge:** For integration, stewardship, and harmony.
   - **The Examining Room:** For testing, questioning, and assessment.

- **The Preparing Room:** For readiness, sincerity, and stripping away before a new phase.
- **The World:** For exposure, trial, and the testing of your character in the public square.

Worked Example:

The Examining Room Imagine you encounter a scathing criticism of your performance. Your instinct is to fight or flee. Instead, you place the criticism in the **Examining Room.** Within this space, the task is not to defend your ego, but to *assess the material.* You hold the criticism at a distance to determine if it contains a truth, fit for your internal lodge, or if it is profane and should be left at the door. You leave the room clearer, regardless of whether you accept the critique.

Step 2: Establishing Authority (Roles)

Once the space is set, you must ask: *Who is the legitimate authority here?* This prevents task-bleed, where you try to solve a structural problem with an emotional stance.

If you're uncertain which Role to assume after identifying your Space (Step 1), return to the interoceptive signal from Step 0. Match the felt sense in your body to the behavioral authority most likely needed.

Where to start: Role Selection by Felt Experience

If the felt sense is...	Starting with...	This Role addresses...
Fragmented attention / constantly hijacked by stimuli	**Tyler**	What is allowed to enter awareness at all
Confusion about what actually happened / facts unclear	**Secretary**	Recording events as they occurred, pattern recognition

If the felt sense is...	Starting with...	This Role addresses...
Depletion / exhaustion / running on empty	**Junior Warden**	Balance between effort and renewal, sustainable rhythm
Tasks that never close / endless unfinished work	**Senior Warden**	Bringing work to proper conclusion, releasing attention
Translation failure / intent gets lost in execution	**Senior Deacon**	Converting abstract values into clear, actionable steps
Misunderstanding / people working at cross-purposes	**Junior Deacon**	Clarifying meaning, ensuring shared understanding
Resource drain / time/ energy misallocated	**Treasurer**	Stewardship of finite resources, alignment with values
Emotional escalation / reactive decisions	**Chaplain**	Restoring equilibrium, returning to composure
Untested assumptions being treated as facts	**Senior Master of Ceremonies**	Verifying claims before they shape action
Unfair conditions / situational misalignment	**Junior Master of Ceremonies**	Aligning context so evaluation is fair
External pressure overriding internal judgment	**Pursuivant**	Filtering illegitimate external influence
Disorientation during unfamiliar transitions	**Guide**	Self-support and context during periods of change
Reactive behavior / decisions driven by circumstance	**Worshipful Master**	Self-leadership, directing attention by chosen values

Important: This table provides a *starting point* based on felt experience. The Worked Example below demonstrates that you may need to shift Roles multiple times before finding the legitimate authority for your specific challenge. Trust the iterative process role-shifting is a feature, not a failure.

The Practice:

1. **Select an Initial Role:** From within your Space, choose the role that seems closest to the work.

2. **Examine Responsibility:** From this role, ask: *What is my actual authority here? What actions are legitimate?*

3. **Shift Deliberately:** If the role feels impotent to solve the problem, shift to another.

Worked Example:

The Mason's Overextension: A brother feels burnt out. He's trying to demonstrate care in all of his relationships.

1. He starts in **Secretary**, and evaluates the care provided, the outcomes created vs. the care requested.

2. He moves to the role of **Chaplain**, trying to care for everyone in alignment with his values. He realizes he has the *desire* to help everyone, even though they didn't ask, and in doing so he has neglected to care for himself.

3. He shifts to the **Junior Warden**. Now, he sees the experience of his own depletion; he recognizes that he is beyond the meridian and needs refreshment.

4. Finally, he assumes the **Senior Warden** role. From this role, he views the problem as a lack of **closure**. The solution isn't more or less care; it is driving toward clarity and closure when commitments are made, and remembering to shift into **Treasurer** and use his **Cabletow** when explicit or implied commitments are evaluated based on available resources.

Step 3: Refining Action (Tools)

Only after you know *where* you are and *who* is acting do you select a Tool. Tools are operative constraints or influences. They don't give you more options; they tell you what you *cannot* do if you wish to remain on the square.

The Practice:

1. **Select the Instrument:** Choose a tool that matches the uncertainty (e.g., the **24 Gauge** for time, the **Compasses** for desire, the **Square** for alignment).

2. **Apply the Constraint:** Allow the tool to restrict your speech or action.

3. **Observe the Result:** Notice what becomes impossible once the tool is applied.

Worked Example:

The 24 Gauge You have a recurring social commitment that leaves you drained. You adopt the **Treasurer** role and apply the **24 Gauge**. The Gauge forces you to account for your 24 hours. As you map it out, you see that this commitment is consuming units of time that belong to your usual vocations or service to a distressed brother. The tool doesn't make the choice for you, but it makes the **disproportion** visible. You can no longer pretend the commitment is without cost.

Step 4: Clarifying Meaning (Systems)

Disagreements often persist because we are processing reality through different lenses. This practice is used when the facts are clear, but the meaning is not.

The Practice:

1. **Hold Facts Constant:** Strip away interpretation.

2. **Filter through the Liberal Arts:** (e.g., Logic, Rhetoric, Geometry)

    - **Logic:** Is this argument internally consistent?

    - **Rhetoric:** What is the *aim* of this communication?

    - **Geometry:** Is the *proportion* of this response correct for the size of the problem?

Worked Example:

Logic and Rhetoric Two brothers disagree on a lodge building project. Both are using **Logic** and their arguments are sound. However, through **Rhetoric**, it becomes clear that one is arguing for historical preservation and the other for future growth. They aren't having a logical fight; they are having a values fight. By naming the system of meaning, the friction is moved from who is right to what are we trying to achieve.

Step 5: Designing for Durability (Elements)

When a plan, a habit, or a relationship appears reasonable but repeatedly fails, the issue is often structural. The Elements, the architectonics of the craft, provide the criteria for evaluating whether a design can carry the weight of lived reality. Use this practice when effort produces fragility rather than strength.

The Practice:

1. **Name the Construction:** Identify the structure under review (e.g., a new professional boundary, a fitness regimen, or a lodge committee plan).

2. **Select a Principle of Evaluation:**
    - **Doric:** Does it prioritize simplicity and essential strength?
    - **Ionic:** Does it balance complexity with wisdom and proportion?
    - **Corinthian:** Does it do all of the above with grace?

3. **Test the Weight:** Ask: *Where does this design rely on perfect conditions to succeed?* Adjust the structure only where the Element indicates a point of failure.

Worked Example:

The Doric Schedule A man creates a meticulously perfect weekly schedule. It is beautiful to look at but collapses the moment a child gets sick or a meeting runs late. By applying the **Doric** lens, he strips away the ornamentation of idealism. He builds in massive margins, simplifies his daily objectives, and prioritizes essential strength over high-resolution planning. The result is less impressive on paper, but it survives the friction of a real week.

Step 6: Interpreting the Field (Foundations)

Foundations describe the enduring patterns of the world that exist regardless of our intentions. This practice is used when you are technically successful but experientially hollow when the work is done, but the alignment is missing.

The Practice:

1. **Identify the Outcome:** Select an experience that feels confusing or unsatisfying.

2. **Apply a Foundational Lens:**
   - **Sun and Moon:** Is there an imbalance between outward exertion (Sun) and inward recovery (Moon)?
   - **The Pavement:** Are you ignoring the inherent duality of the situation; the black and white of joy and sorrow or struggle and achievement?
   - **As Above, So Below:** Does your external action mirror your internal state, or is there a fundamental leak between the two?

3. **Orient, Don't Fix:** Record the insight without trying to repair it immediately. Orientation must precede adjustment.

Worked Example:

As Above, So Below: A man struggles with his ego. He is deeply skilled and profoundly capable and pays homage to his superiors to which he feels obligated to appear grateful. His gratitude is only skin deep and his behavior reflects this with insincere gift-giving and obsequious platitudes. In reflection, he realizes that he intellectually is grateful, but not emotionally so; thus his internal feelings and outward behavior are mismatched.

Step 7: Orienting the Path (Milestones)

Milestones are the ultimate handrails. They help you determine if the *kind* of work you are doing is appropriate for where you are. They prevent the Rough Ashlar from pretending to be Perfect and the Perfect Ashlar from becoming an idol of ego.

The Practice:

1. **Name the Aspiration:** What is the specific goal or project?

2. **Locate the Tension:** Ask:

   - Where is this work still raw and unformed? (**Rough Ashlar**)

   - Where has it been proven and squared? (**Perfect Ashlar**)

   - How does this contribute to a coherence larger than myself? (**The Temple**)

3. **Direct the Effort:** Match your effort to the Milestone. Practice patience where things are raw; practice stewardship where things are refined.

Worked Example:

The New Leader A man is promoted to a role that demands high-level decision-making. He determines that he wants to enhance his skills. By holding the **Ashlars** in tension, he realizes that while his *outcomes* meet or exceed expectations and serves as a Perfect Ashlar, his *team* holds him in contempt for his inhuman treatment to achieve these results. By naming this he accepts the need for the judicious application of his Fellowcraft Apron, to improve his leadership skills while still standing firmly in his ability to perform well.

Quick Triage: The 60-Second Initial Engagement

When the Knock of distress occurs, the goal is to reach **Phase 3** as quickly as possible to apply a constraint before a reactive behavior is manifest.

Scenario A: The Unfair Critique (Professional)

Step 0: The Knock: You feel a hot flush in the face and a tightening in the jaw after an email.

Step 1: The Space: Declare the **Examining Room**. This is not about your worth; it is about assessing the data of the critique.

Step 2: The Role: Assume the **Secretary**. Your only job right now is to record the facts: What was actually said, and what is the evidence for it?

Step 3: The Tool: Apply the **Square**. Does this feedback meet the square of your professional standards? If so, integrate it. If not, it is profane and stays outside.

Scenario B: The Burnt Out Parent/Partner (Relational)

Step 0: The Knock: A feeling of heavy lethargy and the impulse to withdraw or snap at a loved one.

Step 1: The Space: Declare the **Lodge**. The goal here is harmony and the restoration of the Sacred Container of the home.

Step 2: The Role: Assume the **Junior Warden**. Your authority is currently over your own vitality and the rhythm of the household.

Step 3: The Tool: Apply the **24-Inch Gauge**. Look at the remaining hours of the day. Apportion time for refreshment immediately, even if only fifteen minutes, to restore the meridian.

Scenario C: The Impulsive Purchase (Internal)

Step 0: The Knock: An urgent, tunnel-vision desire to acquire a new item to solve a temporary feeling of inadequacy.

Step 1: The Space: Declare the **Preparing Room**. You are at a threshold. Strip away the metallic substances of ego-status before proceeding.

Step 2: The Role: Assume the **Treasurer**. Your authority is the stewardship of finite resources against stated values.

Step 3: The Tool: Apply the **Compasses**. Circumscribe the desire. Set a boundary (e.g., a 48-hour waiting period) to see if the impulse remains within the proportion of your life.

Applying Steps 5 through 7 (The Architectural Review)

Once the immediate heat of the situation has been managed by the first three steps, the Mason uses the remaining steps to ensure the fix is not just a patch but a structural improvement.

Step 4 (Systems): Ask, Am I using the appropriate systemic language to solve the problem?

Step 5 (Elements): Ask, Is the solution I just set appropriate or is it too complex to maintain?

Step 6 (Foundations): Ask, Does this situation reveal a disharmony with the way the world actually works?

Step 7 (Milestones): Ask, Is the friction I'm feeling just the 'Roughness' of a new (skill) that I must be patient with?

Closing the Work: The Operative Result

The *Operative Protocol* is the mechanism that prevents freemasonry from becoming a purely aesthetic pursuit. Without a method for application, the symbols remain ornaments, beautiful to look at, but incapable of holding weight. By moving through these steps, the Mason performs the essential labor of speculative-to-operative translation.

When you name the space, you arrest the momentum of reactive habit. When you assume the role, you reclaim your agency from the grip of impulse. When you apply the tool, you subject your will to the discipline of a higher principle.

The result of this work is not just an improved situation, but a refined man. Each time you run the protocol, you are squaring a piece of your own character, ensuring that when it is finally placed in the temple of your life, it is fit, reliable, and capable of supporting the stones around it. The intent of these steps are there to ensure that as you navigate the complexities of the world, you remain grounded in the reality of the work.

The impossibility of the perfect ashlar

The *Operative Protocol* is an evaluative process, not a linear path. You may enter at the level of a **Tool**, realize you are in the wrong **Space**, and have to return to the start. It may take several attempts to identify the best role to start in to evaluate your specific situation. This process isn't about a single correct answer, or even driving to a specific outcome - it's about adopting a mindset of continuous improvement and conscious development. The work here is perpetual, recursive, and will take a lifetime.

Quick Reference:

Step	Function	Operative Question
0	The Knock	What is my body signaling?
1	Spaces	Where does this work belong?
2	Roles	Who has authority to act?
3	Tools	What are the constraints?
4	Systems	Is the meaning clear?
5	Elements	Is the structure durable?
6	Foundations	How does this work fit?
7	Milestones	Where am I on the path?

PART FOUR: Social Application & Mentorship

The Porch of the Temple: Guidance for the Non-Initiated

While Freemasonry is traditionally a tiled experience conducted within a physical lodge, the tools of symbolic self-development are universal instruments for any individual seeking a purposeful life. If you are not a member of a lodge, you must first establish your own practice to build the necessary intellectual scaffolding.

Building Your Mental Lodge

Before applying the *Operative Protocol*, the layperson (or the Mason returning to the basics) requires a firm grasp of the grammar of the craft. While ritual practice varies by jurisdiction, these resources provide sufficient symbolic vocabulary to engage with the operative framework presented in this book.

Freemasons for Dummies (Hodapp, 2021): This is the essential modern primer for understanding the sociological and historical context of the fraternity.

Duncan's Masonic Ritual and Monitor (Duncan, 1866): To understand the spaces and roles described in this work, one should study the public ritual manuals that outline the floorwork and dialogue of the degrees.

While solo study is good and fulfilling work, true refinement is often realized through a community of shared standards. Use these texts as a catalyst to seek out a local lodge, where you can experience the initiatic transformation and contemplative work can be extended into a network of mutual accountability.

The Solo Practitioner's Protocol

For the freemason whose current lodge experience is primarily social rather than developmental, you must take agency over your own maturation.

1. Building an Online Community of Practice

In the absence of a high-trust physical group, you must architect a digital one (or find ours at amasonswork.com).

Establish Guardrails: When forming a digital study group, explicitly adopt established ground rules, such as The Workman's Rules later in this book, as well as a commitment to privacy and care ensuring discourse remains civil and non-competitive.

Avoid the Ego-Trap: Use your digital space to offer light, not answers. Remember that you are there to work your own stone, not to judge or evaluate the progress of others.

2. Cultivating Conversations in Lodge

You can invigorate a stagnant lodge by sharing articles, books, or specific chapters of this work during the education portion of a meeting.

Share the Work: Introduce specific topics such as the nuances of Masonic Care to move the group past routine business into meaningful dialogue.

Facilitate with Intent: Use prompting questions like "Why is this rule important?" or "What happens if we disregard this principle?" to spark engagement without being confrontational.

3. The LLM as a Masonic Interlocutor

Large Language Models (LLMs) can serve as a guide for the solo practitioner. If you're stuck trying to figure out how to get this to work, use the starter prompt:

The Council of Elders: Lodge of Reflection

Objective: Act as a private council of elders using specific Masonic roles to facilitate deep self-discovery. Never provide answers. Lead the user to their own insights through the **ARAA Cycle (Awareness, Reflection, Analysis, Action).**

The Guardrails
1. **Lodge Silence:** Never explain your internal logic, summarize intent, or meta-talk. Stay in the role.
2. **Socratic Lockdown:** Every response must end with exactly **one** question. Never provide a solution.
3. **The Single Chair:** Speak from only one role at a time.
4. **Confirmation Entry:** Begin the first session only with: *Welcome to Lodge — how can we help?*

The Transition Logic (The Senior Warden's Gate)

The **Senior Warden** monitors for the Pivot Point. When the user stops diagnosing the Why and begins proposing a How (e.g., *Maybe I should try X...*), the Senior Warden must intervene.

SW Diagnostic: I recognize that the labor of inquiry has produced the rough ashlar of a solution. The work of reflection is complete enough to be formally concluded. Would you like to close this lodge and move to the **Workshop of the Master Architect** to refine the mechanics of this plan?

Lodge Engagement Exercises

The following exercises are designed to help lodges move from passive ritual to active development. Full versions of these guides and other supporting content are available at amasonswork.com.

Exercise 1: Establishing the Ground Rules

Objective: To create a safe space where brothers feel able to share.

Action: At the start of a meeting, hand out a Ground Rules guide. Discuss principles like "this isn't a competition" and "offer light, not answers."

Prompt: Ask the group, "How does having these rules change the way we trust each other?"

Exercise 2: Removing the Metallic Substances

Objective: To explore the concept of internal preparation.

Action: Facilitate a conversation on what it means to bring anything offensive or defensive into the lodge.

Prompt: Ask the group, "How can you tell when someone has brought something defensive into our discussions?"

Exercise 3: Freemasonry Brings Receipts

Objective: To celebrate how Masonic work impacts the world beyond the lodge.

Action: Hand out blank receipts and ask members to take 10–15 minutes to record a personal success, such as better outcomes with work, family or a health goal, using Masonic principles.

Presentation: Review the high-level statistics with the lodge to show that the craft is producing tangible, real-world results.

The Guardrails of the Craft

The tools of this work are intended for the self, but their use inevitably changes how we move among others. When self-development tools are misapplied socially, they risk becoming instruments of correction and manipulation rather than formation. To prevent this, all collaborative work is governed by

The Workman's Rules:

1. **Use your Trowel:** Prioritize cohesion over correction.

2. **Don't Spread Salt:** Unskillful or hurtful speech corrodes relationships.

3. **Work your own stone:** Insight does not grant jurisdiction. Your work ends at your own borders.

4. **All work is stone work:** All suffering contains the opportunity for development.

5. **You'll work the same stone until you get it right:** Avoidance is merely a delay.

6. **Never judge your work relative to someone else's:** Comparison is a distortion.

7. **Never judge someone else's work relative to your own:** Hierarchy is an error.

8. **You can't work another man's stone, but you can lighten his load:** Mentorship is load-bearing, not direction-giving.

9. **Right tool, Right place, Right time:** Restraint is as vital as technique.

Mentorship as Presence

True mentorship is often an act of *presence*, not instruction. In this mode, the mentor is a stabilizing presence, not a source of answers. Their role is to prevent the worker from abandoning the stone when the friction of formation becomes uncomfortable.

This is quiet work. It involves listening without urgency and asking questions that do not lead. The mentor does not interpret the work; they protect the conditions that allow the worker to complete his own course. It is an act of trust in the process, measured by how little the mentor needs to say.

Functional Mirroring: The Borrowed Apron

In incidental mentorship, a mentor may temporarily borrow a lodge role to help another clarify his experience without assuming ownership of the problem. This is done explicitly and with great restraint.

> *Before entering any conversation where you might help in this way it is absolutely vital and necessary to ask "Are you looking to vent, or would you like to approach this Masonically?"*

The Mentorship Script: The Master's Question

To help with the social application, here is how a mentor bridges the gap between a Brother's distress and the Work:

Brother: I'm just so frustrated with how things are going at work. Nobody listens to me.

Mentor: I can hear the weight of that. Before we dive in, **are you looking to vent, or would you like to approach this Masonically?**

Brother: Masonically. I need to get my head right.

Mentor: Understood. Let's move this into the

Examining Room [Step 1]. I'm going to put on the
Secretary's apron [Step 2]. Tell me the facts of the
last interaction: what was said, specifically?

This script transforms a complaint into a *stone working* session,
where the mentor is simply the one holding the lamp while the
Brother handles the gavel.

Worked Example: The Burden of Imposter Syndrome

Brother: I don't think I'm qualified for my success. It feels
like I'm getting away with something.

Mentor: *[The mentor resists the urge to reassure, which would
misapply the Trowel by invalidating the Brother's current
felt reality]* You want to vent or would you like some help
figuring things out?

Brother: I think I'd like some help if you're okay with that?

Mentor: *[Assuming the Role of the Secretary]* Let me put
on my **Secretary** apron for a moment. What facts match
what you're feeling, which achievements in specific are you
referring to?

Brother: *[The Brother lists his successes]*.

Mentor: Are there facts indicating the opposite? Places
you're dropping the ball or avoidable mistakes?

Brother: No, not really.

Mentor: *[The Secretary concludes the record. The facts are now
distinct from the feeling]* Let me put on the **Chaplain's** apron
for a second. Separating the facts from the feelings, how
does the feeling that you're an imposter benefit you?

Brother: I'm not sure... but I've got this perpetual anxiety.
It's like if I stop proving myself, I'll be exposed. I never
considered that to be a benefit, but I guess it's helping me
stay focused?

Mentor: What is the cost of that belief?

Brother: That I never rest.

Mentor: *[The belief is named; the mentor shifts to the Junior Warden to address energy]* Wearing the **Junior Warden's** apron now, what is this cost doing to your life right now?

Brother: *[The Brother recognizes the toll on his sleep, patience, and joy]*.

Mentor: What happens to the work when those costs go unpaid?

Brother: *[The Brother sees the inevitable decline]*. I guess my work quality will go down and all the stuff I'm worried about now will probably start to happen.

Mentor: [The mentor takes the apron off. He has not given advice. He has simply held the mirror of the lodge's roles up to the brother's life until the brother could see his own Unjust Master for what it was.] How will you move forward knowing what you know now?

Brother: I'm not sure, but I do have a stronger sense for what's going on. Thanks for the help!

There's a good chance that you could write examples like this for the work you've already done in your life; some misconception that was dissolved by switching perspectives. You might try that as an exercise in readiness to help someone else learn from your efforts.

Additional Mentoring Examples

Mentoring Exercise 1: The Tyler's Threshold

Objective: To help a Brother identify and gate external noise that disrupts his internal work.

The Role: The mentor adopts the role of the **Tyler**.

The Action: The Brother presents a current stressor or distraction. The mentor asks: Is this stimulus 'properly clothed' to enter your lodge right now? and does this distraction have a legitimate 'credential' to claim your attention, or is it an intruder?

The Goal: To help the Brother realize he has the authority to deny entry to thoughts or demands that do not serve his current developmental focus.

Mentoring Exercise 2: The Senior Deacon's Translation

Objective: To bridge the gap between a brother's high-level ideals and his concrete, daily actions.

The Role: The mentor adopts the role of the **Senior Deacon**.

The Action: The brother identifies a core value (e.g., Integrity). The mentor asks: How do we translate this 'command' from the East into a message the 'workmen' in your daily life can understand? and what does this principle look like when it moves from a thought into a physical step?

The Goal: To practice the translation of abstract Masonic light into actionable, operative behavior.

PART FIVE: The Masonic Symbols

The symbols and interpretations presented in this section
are the perspectives of the author alone and are rooted in the
specific masonic ritual of Pennsylvania, USA. While these
symbols form a coherent operating system for self-development,
they are not intended to be dogmatic nor exhaustive. They are
functional lenses meant to structure attention and coordinate
behavior, rather than static definitions to be memorized.

Readers are strongly encouraged to rewrite, expand, or discard
these interpretations to better serve their own developmental
needs. The library of symbols is less important than its ability
to provide diverse perspectives and facilitate the Awareness-
Reflection-Analysis-Action (ARAA) cycle. If you find more
resonance in a different symbolic set (such as the cycles of the
natural world, other craft traditions, or modern psychological
frameworks) you are invited to integrate them into this protocol.

When using these symbols for social application or mentorship,
it is vital to remember the concept of *Protective Abstraction*.
This allows individuals to discuss personal challenges without
triggering defensiveness. However, because symbols can be
highly personal, you should always calibrate your definitions
with your conversational partner. Before beginning Stone
Work with another, ensure you are speaking the same symbolic

language so that the intent of the communication survives the transmission.

The ultimate goal is not the mastery of the symbols themselves, but the intentional refinement of consciousness. These are working tools, and like any hammer or gauge, their value is found entirely in their application to the unprocessed stone of daily life.

A Functional Taxonomy for Operative Interpretation

The symbols of the craft can be used to form a coherent operating system for self-development. They are not isolated emblems, but functional lenses through which an individual examines identity, action, structure, and purpose. By grouping these symbols according to their operative function, we clarify the specific inquiry each supports.

This taxonomy organizes the symbolic vocabulary into seven distinct dimensions of human engagement.

I. Spaces (Containers for Effort) Spaces define the environments in which work occurs. They do not perform the work; they permit it. These symbols identify the contexts of transformation from the sacred container of the lodge to the examining room of the conscience, and clarify what each environment demands of the man within it.

II. Roles (Identity and Stance) Roles describe the identities and responsibilities an individual assumes when engaging with experience. These symbols represent functional positions; learner, steward, guide, or protector, and clarify the necessary orientation and obligation required for the work at hand.

III. Tools (Means of Work) Tools are the operative implements that regulate conduct and surface insight. They are used to investigate a situation through disciplined technique squaring an action, circumscribing a desire, or structuring the allocation of effort. They also include indicators of distortion, such as base metals or valuables, which reveal internal attachments and misalignments.

IV. Systems of Meaning (Cognitive Disciplines) Systems represent the intellectual structures through which we discover and communicate meaning. Drawing from the liberal arts and sciences, these symbols provide the methods by which clarity emerges, whether through the logic of an argument, the proportion of a design, or the harmony of a relationship.

V. Elements (Architectonics) Elements describe the structural principles underlying effective design. These symbols such as the orders of architecture or the pillars of the porch provide the criteria for evaluating whether a life or a project is fit for purpose, stable, and elegant in its construction.

VI. Foundations (Metaphysical Patterns) Foundations describe the enduring truths and cosmic patterns that shape human experience. These symbols articulate the fundamental realities; labor and rest, duality and unity, cause and consequence, within which all work is conducted. They orient the Mason toward the unchanging principles governing existence.

VII. Milestones (Developmental Trajectory) Milestones describe the movement from potential to refinement. These symbols mark the stages of a man's labor and the ultimate aim of his life. They serve as a map for the path from the rough ashlar of raw potential to the temple of a coherent, meaningful life.

Using the Taxonomy

The purpose of this taxonomy is to move from abstract study to precise inquiry. When confronting a challenge, the Mason selects a symbolic lens to clarify his perspective:

- **What environment** am I in, and what does it require? (Spaces)
- **Who must I be** in this moment? (Roles)

- **How should I act** or investigate? (Tools)
- **How should I think** about what is emerging? (Systems)
- **How should I plan** to make a solution that lasts? (Elements)
- **How can I leverage** the way the world already works to make this outcome smoother? (Foundations)
- **How does this fit** in the scope of my life? (Milestones)

Each symbol in the following section is analyzed through a three-fold lens:

- **Intrinsic:** The practical, behavioral application (What is the work?).

- **Extrinsic:** The relational fit within a larger system (How does this connect?).

- **Integrative:** The transformative capacity of the tool on the man's consciousness (What is the deeper truth?).

The designs featured throughout are intended for visualization and are sourced from the masonic symbols set at our website http://amasonswork.com. Because masonic traditions vary by jurisdiction and preference, we encourage you to treat this as a living toolkit; one to be customized through practice, refined by reflection, and discussed within your Lodge.

Spaces

Spaces define the environments in which work occurs. They do not perform the work; they permit it. These symbols identify the contexts of transformation from the sacred container of the lodge to the examining room of the conscience, and clarify what each environment demands of the man within it.

The Lodge

The Space of Collective Coherence

The Lodge is a bounded environment governed by rules, roles, and ritual order. Its primary function is to separate ordinary life from purposeful work, creating the conditions where attention, conduct, and meaning are held to a higher standard than the profane world outside.

The Lenses

Intrinsic (Personal): The mental faculty that creates an intentional internal space setting aside distraction, ego, and urgency so focused growth can occur.

Extrinsic (Interpersonal): The coordination of individual differences through shared rules and purpose, allowing trust to form without requiring absolute agreement.

Integrative (Systemic): The principle that transformation occurs within intentional containers; a shared consciousness that supports development beyond individual effort.

The ARAA Sequence:

Awareness - When to Use This Symbol

Identify when the work lacks a proper container:

- Work feels scattered, unfocused, or lacking a clear boundary from daily distractions.
- Individual effort lacks the reinforcement of a shared standard or supportive community.
- The meaning of the work is eroding under the weight of routine or excessive informality.
- Group identity is weakening into a merely social gathering without a developmental center.
- Transformation is being sought through information alone, without the structure of a dedicated space.

Reflection - Diagnostic Questions

Turn the gaze toward the quality of your current working environment:

- What specific boundaries currently make this space functional for the work I am doing?

- How am I personally participating in maintaining the coherence and focus of this group?

- What specific behaviors belong inside this intentional space and which must be left at the door?

- What specific work becomes possible here that is simply not possible in the World outside?

Analysis - Failure Modes

Analyze the potential for the distortion of the sacred container:

Overuse (The Dogmatist/Ritualist): Becoming enamored with the sacred nature of the space while losing touch with its practical application; treating symbols as literal rules rather than tools.

Underuse (The Profane Worker): Attempting to coordinate complex labor without a shared integral intent; treating the work as a transaction, resulting in fragmented language and lack of trust.

Action - Use It Now

Manifest the insight through disciplined behavior:

Before entering your next meeting or collaborative effort, consciously mark the transition set a clear intention, respect the agreed boundaries, and participate fully in maintaining the focus of the space.

The Examining Room

The Space of Epistemic Discernment

The Examining Room is a space designated for verification, where credentials are tested and understanding is assessed according to established standards. Its function is to filter entry into higher levels of responsibility through lawful, procedural discernment rather than personal bias or familiarity.

The Lenses

Intrinsic (Personal): The mental faculty that tests internal claims and beliefs against objective standards before accepting them as true or ready.

Extrinsic (Interpersonal): The recognition of readiness by others, where admission to a role is acknowledged through verification rather than self-declaration.

Integrative (Systemic): The principle that systems remain coherent through lawful filtering, preventing the dilution of meaning and the erosion of standards.

The ARAA Sequence:

Awareness - When to Use This Symbol

Identify when entry or progress is being granted without verification:

- Entry into a role or project is being granted based on assumption, proximity, or good vibes.
- Standards for readiness are being applied inconsistently depending on the person or the pressure of the moment.
- Knowledge or skill is being claimed but has not been demonstrated in a controlled environment.
- Social familiarity is bypassing the necessary process of verifying actual qualification.

Awareness - When to Use This Symbol (continued)

- The integrity of a system is eroding because of a convenient lack of scrutiny.

Reflection - Diagnostic Questions

Assess the criteria for progression in your current context:

- What specific standard actually governs entry into this role or level of trust?

- What tangible evidence currently demonstrates readiness to proceed to the next step?

- Where might my familiarity with a person or idea be replacing my duty of verification?

- What must be definitively known, not merely intended, before this work can move forward?

Analysis - Failure Modes

Analyze the potential for the distortion of the testing process:

Overuse (The Hyper-Critic/Inquisitor): Turning the testing of ideas into an end in itself; subjecting every thought to such extreme scrutiny that you paralyze action and create a culture of suspicion.

Underuse (The Credulous/Blind Believer): Allowing ideas or people into your internal Lodge without any verification; assuming shared identity is a substitute for competence.

Action - Use It Now

Manifest the insight through disciplined behavior:

Before granting access to responsibility, trust, or authority, either to yourself or others, verify readiness against explicit criteria, independent of relationship or urgency.

The Preparing Room

The Space of Intentional Formation

The Preparing Room is a space of transition where an individual is separated from the ordinary world to be oriented toward the threshold ahead. It is not where work is done, but where the *worker* is prepared by quieting noise and adopting a posture of receptivity and humility.

The Lenses

Intrinsic (Personal): The mental faculty that suspends habit, quiets internal noise, and prepares the self to be examined and eventually changed.

Extrinsic (Interpersonal): The adoption of a posture of vulnerability before the community, signaling respect for the process rather than confidence in the outcome.

Integrative (Systemic): The principle that formation requires an emptying before shaping; systems that rush entry without preparation absorb unexamined habits.

The ARAA Sequence:

Awareness - When to Use This Symbol

Identify when the transition into new work is too abrupt:

- Entry into a new phase of life or work feels rushed, casual, or lacking in gravity.
- Readiness is being assumed as a given rather than being cultivated through pause and reflection.
- The prospect of being examined or tested feels like a threat rather than an appropriate step.
- Existing habits or a loud ego are dominating your posture as you approach a new threshold.
- Formation is being skipped entirely in favor of immediate validation or performance.

Reflection - Diagnostic Questions

Assess your current state of readiness for the work ahead:

- What specific distractions or assumptions must I set aside before I can proceed?

- Am I currently oriented to be examined and changed, or am I merely looking to advance?

- What metallic defenses or distractions are still active in my mind right now?

- What specific posture or state of mind best honors the seriousness of the threshold I am facing?

Analysis - Failure Modes

Analyze the potential for the distortion of preparation:

Overuse (The Perpetual Seeker): Becoming addicted to the cleansing process; spending all your time preparing and shedding weight but never building the muscle of the Work.

Underuse (The Impatient Egotist): Trying to enter the work with your defenses and biases still attached; refusing the pause required for humility and distorting the Work as a result.

Action - Use It Now

Manifest the insight through disciplined behavior:

Before entering your next consequential conversation or role, create a brief preparing space; pause, remove distractions, and consciously adopt a posture of readiness.

The World

The Space of Practical Application

The World is the uncontrolled environment beyond the lodge where actions have real-world consequences and results cannot be insulated by ritual. It is the ultimate testing ground where character is proven by how well principles are integrated with the messy reality of circumstance and feedback.

The Lenses

Intrinsic (Personal): The mental faculty that integrates principles with real-world circumstances, allowing learning to occur through consequence.

Extrinsic (Interpersonal): The interaction with others that reveals blind spots; impact is measured by reality rather than by one's own internal intent.

Integrative (Systemic): The principle of praxis; that the measure of truth is found in the sustained function of a system within uncontrolled environments.

The ARAA Sequence:

Awareness - When to Use This Symbol

Identify when growth has become stagnant or purely theoretical:

- Valuable insights are being gathered in the lodge or in study, but they are not translating into actual behavior.

- Core principles remain theoretical or perfect because they have never been tested by friction.

- External feedback is being avoided, dismissed, or ignored to protect a self-image.

- Personal growth has stalled despite a significant amount of learning or reading.

- Your identity as a person of integrity is confined only to protected or safe contexts.

Reflection - Diagnostic Questions

Assess the field test of your current principles:

- Where exactly must this principle be applied right now for it to be truly tested?

- What specific feedback am I currently receiving from my reality and my results?

- Where does my actual impact in the world diverge from my original internal intention?

- What adjustment in my behavior does the current consequence of my actions require?

Analysis - Failure Modes

Analyze the potential for the distortion of engagement:

Overuse (The Habitual Reactionary): Living entirely in the noise; having an identity that is a mere composite of external pressures and unexamined impulses.

Underuse (The Hermit/Isolationist): Fearing the world so much that you refuse to engage; treating the lodge as a hideout rather than a workshop for world-shaping skills.

Action - Use It Now

Manifest the insight through disciplined behavior:

Take one principle or habit you value and apply it deliberately in an uncontrolled real-world context; observe the outcome and adjust your posture without defensiveness.

Roles

Roles describe the identities and responsibilities an individual assumes when engaging with experience. These symbols represent functional positions; learner, steward, guide, or protector, and clarify the necessary orientation and obligation required for the work at hand.

The Freemason

The Role of the Conscious Participant

The role of the Freemason is the foundational orientation of the entire system; it represents the transition from a passive observer of life to an active participant in a structured project of character refinement.

The Lenses

Intrinsic (Personal): The deliberate act of orienting one's attention and actions around a chosen ethical frame rather than habitual reaction.

Extrinsic (Interpersonal): The embodiment of presence-in-relation, stabilizing interactions by maintaining a posture of mutual regard and shared obligation.

Integrative (Systemic): The recognition that human development is a cultivated project, with the individual serving as the essential unit of transformation for the entire system.

The ARAA Sequence:

Awareness - When to Use This Symbol

Identify the environmental cues that signal a loss of orientation:

- Participation feels routine or disengaged rather than intentional.
- Decisions are made without reference to shared values.
- Attendance replaces involvement, and presence becomes nominal.
- Responsibility is deferred to officers rather than owned personally.
- The purpose of the lodge feels vague or taken for granted.

Reflection - Diagnostic Questions

Turn the gaze inward to assess your current posture:

- How am I currently positioning myself in relation to work?

- What values am I orienting my actions around right now?

- In what ways am I actively participating, rather than merely attending?

- Where have I outsourced responsibility instead of assuming it?

Analysis - Failure Modes

Analyze the potential for distortion and internal misalignment:

Overuse (Performative Identity): Treating Freemasonry as a label or an aesthetic to be displayed rather than a labor to be performed. You are in love with the idea of being a Mason, using the identity to mask a lack of actual internal transformation.

Underuse (Passive Conformity): Confusing alignment with mere obedience. You wait for direction rather than establishing your own orientation, reducing your presence to a procedural compliance that lacks any developmental heat.

Action - Use It Now

Manifest the insight through disciplined behavior:

Before your next meeting or decision, pause and identify what you are orienting toward; approval, convenience, habit, or principle, and adjust one concrete action accordingly.

The Worshipful Master

The Role of Intentional Governance

The Worshipful Master represents the organizing center of leadership, charged with directing work and maintaining the standards and creating space that allow a system to function coherently. Without this function, effort fragments and intention loses its direction, regardless of the worker's skill.

The Lenses

Intrinsic (Personal): The faculty of self-leadership that regulates internal impulses and directs attention in alignment with chosen values.

Extrinsic (Interpersonal): The management of authority and presence to set a stable climate where others can engage, listen, and contribute.

Integrative (Systemic): The principle that order arises from the intentional leadership of values and standards within both individuals and organizations.

The ARAA Sequence:

Awareness - When to Use This Symbol

Identify the environmental cues that signal a failure of governance:

- Decisions feel reactive to circumstances rather than guided by intention.
- Authority is present in title but inconsistently applied to the work.
- Internal conflict or emotional reactivity undermines external leadership.
- Standards of conduct are articulated but not visibly embodied.
- Long-term purpose is being sacrificed for short-term comfort or avoidance.

Reflection - Diagnostic Questions

Turn the gaze inward to assess your current leadership of self and others:

- What is currently governing my attention and my decisions in this moment?

- Where do I need to reassert standards, either internally for myself, or externally for the group?

- How is my current internal state shaping the climate I am creating for others?

- Am I leading the situation deliberately, or merely responding to the nearest pressure?

Analysis - Failure Modes

Analyze the potential for distortion in how authority is exercised:

Overuse (Internal Tyranny): Substituting positional authority for personal discipline; you attempt to govern others as a way to avoid the harder work of regulating your own reactivity and impulses.

Underuse (Abdication): Avoiding necessary correction or standard-setting to maintain a false peace; you allow the lodge of your life to drift into disorder because you fear the friction of asserting a boundary.

Action - Use It Now

Manifest the insight through disciplined behavior:

Before your next decision or interaction, pause and identify what principle you intend to govern by, then adjust one response so your internal posture and external action align.

Senior Deacon

The Role of Translation between Intent and Execution

The Senior Deacon is responsible for the transmission of meaning, ensuring that intent is converted into usable guidance without distortion as it moves from authority to action. This role preserves the coherence of the system by ensuring that what is meant is exactly what is understood.

The Lenses

Intrinsic (Personal): The mental faculty that translates abstract values and internal decisions into clear, actionable steps for the self.

Extrinsic (Interpersonal): The function of interpretation that reduces friction between parties by ensuring meaning survives across different contexts.

Integrative (Systemic): The principle that systems function only when meaning survives transmission and intent propagates accurately through the structure.

The ARAA Sequence:

Awareness - When to Use This Symbol

Identify the environmental cues that signal a loss of meaning in transmission:

- Instructions are delivered but frequently misunderstood or misapplied.
- Final outcomes consistently diverge from the original stated intent.
- Rework is common because tasks were performed based on a misinterpretation.
- Individuals act in good faith but find themselves working at cross purposes.
- Clarification is repeatedly required long after decisions have supposedly been made.

Reflection - Diagnostic Questions

Assess how clearly you are translating intent into action:

- What is the actual, underlying intent behind this instruction or decision?

- How can I express this so it is understood by the recipient without distortion?

- Where might the meaning be getting lost between the intention and the final execution?

- Am I adding personal editorializing or interpretation that does not belong to the original intent?

Analysis - Failure Modes

Analyze how translation is being corrupted:

Overuse (Internal Advocacy): Injecting personal preference or editorializing the translation of intent; you use nuance to soften or change a difficult principle to suit your comfort.

Underuse (Oversimplification): Stripping away the complexity of an intent to avoid the effort of clear communication; you assume understanding without confirmation, leading to systemic fracture.

Action - Use It Now

Manifest the insight through disciplined behavior:

Take one recent decision or directive you are responsible for communicating, restate its intent in concrete terms, and confirm it is understood as intended before proceeding.

Senior Warden

The Role of Conclusion and Equitable Distribution

The Senior Warden oversees the completion of labor, ensuring that work is brought to a proper close and that rewards are distributed fairly. This role prevents endless, unresolved activity by recognizing when effort has sufficiently achieved its purpose.

The Lenses

Intrinsic (Personal): The mental faculty that determines when a phase of work is complete enough to release attention and move toward rest.

Extrinsic (Interpersonal): The safeguarding of fairness through acknowledgment and compensation proportionate to an individual's actual contribution.

Integrative (Systemic): The principle that systems require closure to maintain harmony, prevent burnout, and preserve clarity about responsibility.

The ARAA Sequence:

Awareness - When to Use This Symbol

Identify the environmental cues that signal a failure to conclude:

- Tasks remain open or active long after their original purpose has been met.
- Effort continues to be expended on a project without any clear ongoing benefit.
- Recognition or reward for labor feels uneven, absent, or disconnected from contribution.
- Transitions between different phases of work are blurred or non-existent.
- Fatigue accumulates in the group because work never feels truly finished.

Reflection - Diagnostic Questions

Assess your ability to bring work to a healthy resolution:

- What specific piece of work is complete enough to be formally concluded right now?

- Where am I currently extending my effort past its point of useful return?

- How is the contribution of those involved being acknowledged or balanced in this moment?

- What needs to be formally closed to allow for a period of renewal or a new beginning?

Analysis - Failure Modes

Analyze the distortion of completion:

Overuse (Stagnation): Ending work prematurely or abandoning tasks before they reach their intended form to escape the weight of accountability.

Underuse (Perpetual Motion): Mistaking mere endurance for effectiveness; you allow unfinished tasks to linger indefinitely because you fear the emptiness after a project is finished.

Action - Use It Now

Manifest the insight through disciplined behavior:

Identify one ongoing task or obligation that has effectively achieved its purpose and formally conclude it, communicate the closure, acknowledge the contributions, and release the remaining effort.

Junior Deacon

The Role of Communication Gating and Neutrality

The Junior Deacon facilitates communication where understanding is most vulnerable, at the points of exchange and coordination between individuals. This role exists to clarify meaning and ensure that shared understanding precedes action, preventing misunderstandings from hardening into errors.

The Lenses

Intrinsic (Personal): The mental faculty that checks comprehension, resolves internal ambiguity, and ensures meaning is solid before proceeding.

Extrinsic (Interpersonal): The maintenance of relational neutrality that supports communication without taking sides or introducing emotional charge.

Integrative (Systemic): The principle that systems depend on clear, undistorted channels of communication to maintain coordination and trust.

The ARAA Sequence:

Awareness - When to Use This Symbol

Identify the environmental cues that signal a communication breakdown:

- People are acting on unverified assumptions rather than a shared understanding.

- Instructions are followed inconsistently across the group despite a general good intent.

- Small, simple misunderstandings are escalating quickly into larger interpersonal issues.

- Communication feels rushed, incomplete, or high-pressure.

- Clarifying questions are treated as an interruption or are actively discouraged.

Reflection - Diagnostic Questions

Assess the quality of clarity in your current interactions:

- What might be assumed by either party but has not been explicitly stated or understood?

- Have all parties involved actually confirmed the same understanding of the task?

- Where could ambiguity in my language or theirs create an unnecessary error later?

- Am I remaining neutral while I clarify this, or am I adding my own emotional interpretation?

Analysis - Failure Modes

Analyze the distortion of clarification:

Overuse (Obstruction): Over-clarifying to the point of stalling momentum; you use neutral questioning as a passive-aggressive tool to delay work you disagree with.

Underuse (Assumption): Avoiding the pause required for clarification to maintain social speed; you value the appearance of momentum over the reality of accuracy.

Action - Use It Now

Manifest the insight through disciplined behavior:

In your next interaction, pause to restate what you believe the other person means and ask for their confirmation before you take any further action.

Junior Warden

The Role of Regulation and Sustainable Rhythm

The Junior Warden is responsible for overseeing periods of refreshment and ensuring that labor is balanced with rest. This role manages energy, desire, and rhythm so that effort remains sustainable and does not degrade into excess or burnout.

The Lenses

Intrinsic (Personal): The mental faculty that monitors internal capacity, sets limits on exertion, and maintains the balance between work and replenishment.

Extrinsic (Interpersonal): The management of a communal rhythm that allows all members to engage fully without experiencing exhaustion or resentment.

Integrative (Systemic): The principle that renewal is a structural necessity for any system to endure rather than collapse under continuous strain.

The ARAA Sequence:

Awareness - When to Use This Symbol

Identify the environmental cues that signal an imbalance of rhythm:

- Fatigue is accumulating in yourself or others without any formal acknowledgment.
- Productivity and focus are fluctuating unpredictably throughout the cycle.
- Rest is treated as a luxury, an indulgence, or is avoided entirely as waste.
- Energy is being expended unevenly, with some individuals in overdrive and others disengaged.
- Short-term impulses or appetites are undermining long-term effectiveness.

Reflection - Diagnostic Questions

Assess your current balance of effort and renewal:

- What internal or external signals indicate that a period of regulation is needed right now?

- How am I currently managing the balance between my output and my replenishment?

- Where is excess, either of work or of indulgence, disrupting my natural rhythm?

- How does my personal lack of regulation affect the tempo and energy of the group?

Analysis - Failure Modes

Analyze the distortion of rest and regulation:

Overuse (Hedonism): Overindulging in refreshment under the guise of self-care; you use the concept of rest to avoid the friction of necessary labor.

Underuse (Burnout): Ignoring limits until you are forced into a halt by total exhaustion; you treat your vitality as an infinite resource rather than a structural one.

Action - Use It Now

Manifest the insight through disciplined behavior:

Notice one pattern of overexertion or indulgence in your current routine and make one small adjustment to restore balance; observe the effect on your energy over the next cycle.

Secretary

The Role of Honest Recollection and Record

The Secretary is responsible for the maintenance of records and the preservation of institutional memory. As a mental function, this role enables pattern recognition by maintaining a reliable account of prior actions and outcomes, ensuring that reflection is grounded in fact rather than mood or retrospective justification.

The Lenses

Intrinsic (Personal): The cognitive discipline of recording events exactly as they occurred, without distortion by emotion, preference, or the pressure to protect one's identity.

Extrinsic (Interpersonal): The maintenance of a shared memory grounded in evidence, which reduces relational projection and defensiveness by anchoring disputes to a factual reference.

Integrative (Systemic): The principle that coherent systems depend on honest data over time to discern meaningful patterns of growth, decline, or failure.

The ARAA Sequence:

Awareness - When to Use This Symbol

Identify the environmental cues that signal a failure of memory or data:

- Decisions are being justified by current feelings rather than evidence of past outcomes.

- The same problems or interpersonal conflicts recur without a clear understanding of their origin.

- Personal or group narratives shift conveniently to avoid discomfort or accountability.

- Trends or progress are being inferred based on anecdotes rather than reliable records.

Reflection - Diagnostic Questions

Assess the honesty and accuracy of your internal and external records:

- What actually happened in this situation, separate from how I feel about it?

- Where might my current emotional state be distorting my recollection of past events?

- What patterns become visible when I look at the actual data of my behavior over time?

- Am I preserving the facts of this situation, or am I protecting a preferred narrative?

Analysis - Failure Modes

Analyze the potential for the corruption of truth through record-keeping:

Overuse (Narrative Manipulation): Selective recording of facts to support a preferred conclusion; using the record as a weapon or a shield rather than a tool for honest inquiry.

Underuse (Selective Memory): Allowing emotion to overwrite factual recollection entirely; treating memory as sufficient while ignoring the objective documentation of habits.

Action - Use It Now

Manifest the insight through disciplined behavior:

Choose a recent event that carries emotional weight and write a neutral, factual account of what occurred; compare this record to your remembered narrative and notice what changes.

Treasurer

The Role of Stewardship and Value Alignment

The Treasurer is responsible for safeguarding and disbursing the resources of the lodge, ensuring that all obligations are met responsibly. Symbolically, this role represents the mental faculty that evaluates cost, worth, and tradeoffs; disciplining desire by ensuring that investments of time, energy, and attention align with stated purpose.

The Lenses

Intrinsic (Personal): The mental faculty that decides which projects, relationships, or desires are worthy of an investment of finite internal resources.

Extrinsic (Interpersonal): The maintenance of ethical exchange and trust by ensuring that contributions are handled fairly and obligations are honored consistently.

Integrative (Systemic): The principle that a system's true priorities are defined by where it allocates its resources rather than its declared ideals.

The ARAA Sequence:

Awareness - When to Use This Symbol

Identify the environmental cues that signal a failure of stewardship:

- Resources (time, money, or energy) are being allocated without clear or consistent criteria.
- Spending or commitment decisions are driven by momentary urgency or external pressure.
- Long-term obligations are being obscured or ignored in favor of short-term gains.
- Trust is eroding within a group regarding the fairness or transparency of resource use.

- You feel constantly overdrawn,
  fatigued, or bankrupt in your energy
  and attention.

Reflection - Diagnostic Questions

Assess your current stewardship of value and resources:

- What am I currently investing my most valuable
  resources in, and why?

- Do these allocations of energy and attention reflect my
  stated values or just momentary pressures?

- Where are hidden costs or debts accumulating in my life
  or my work?

- What boundaries need to be enforced right now to
  protect my long-term structural health?

Analysis - Failure Modes

Analyze the potential for the distortion of value:

*Overuse (Transactionalism): Confusing generosity with a
lack of discernment; using resources purely to appease others
and avoid conflict until you are personally bankrupt.*

*Underuse (Indiscipline): Allocating resources without
criteria; avoiding the difficult tradeoffs required to
maintain a coherent life in the hope that more will solve the
problem.*

Action - Use It Now

Manifest the insight through disciplined behavior:

Review one recent allocation of your time or attention;
assess whether it reflects your stated priorities and adjust
your next allocation to better align with what you claim to
value.

Chaplain

The Role of Centering and Equilibrium

The Chaplain offers reflections and invocations to mark transitions and stabilize the emotional tone of the lodge. This role represents the mental faculty that reorients attention toward meaning and proportion when emotions, pressures, or distractions threaten to overwhelm judgment.

The Lenses

Intrinsic (Personal): The mental faculty that restores internal equilibrium and returns the self to a state of composure before proceeding with action.

Extrinsic (Interpersonal): The provision of a stable emotional anchor that reduces reactivity in others and creates the conditions for respectful, grounded engagement.

Integrative (Systemic): The principle that meaning sustains systems under strain, preventing them from being driven entirely by fear, urgency, or fatigue.

The ARAA Sequence:

Awareness - When to Use This Symbol

Identify the environmental cues that signal a loss of equilibrium:

- Emotional intensity or heat is starting to overwhelm thoughtful decision-making.
- Interactions are escalating quickly into conflict or feeling emotionally charged and reactive.
- The primary purpose of the work is being overshadowed by urgency, fear, or friction.
- People (or parts of yourself) are struggling to regain composure after a disruption or setback.
- Reflection and pause are being treated as a delay rather than a necessary support.

Reflection - Diagnostic Questions

Assess your current state of centeredness and perspective:

- What specific action or thought would help restore my internal steadiness right now?

- Where has my emotion or reactive impulse overtaken my broader perspective?

- What shared purpose or core value needs to be recalled in this specific moment?

- Am I acting from a place of centered awareness, or am I merely reacting to the current pressure?

Analysis - Failure Modes

Analyze the potential for the distortion of centering:

Overuse (Avoidance): Using reflection or the pursuit of calm as a way to avoid taking necessary but uncomfortable action; imposing calm on others as a means of control.

Underuse (Brittleness): Treating pause and meaning as abstract luxuries; allowing yourself to be driven entirely by urgency until you fracture under pressure.

Action - Use It Now

Manifest the insight through disciplined behavior:

When you notice emotional escalation, in yourself or a group, pause intentionally, take one steady breath, and recall the specific purpose guiding the situation before you respond.

Senior Master of Ceremonies

The Role of Epistemic Verification

The Senior Master of Ceremonies is responsible for formal admission and examination, serving as the safeguard of the lodge by ensuring that claims of membership are tested before acceptance. This role represents the cognitive faculty of verification; the discipline of evaluating whether a belief or self-concept is warranted before it is allowed to shape judgment.

The Lenses

Intrinsic (Personal): The cognitive faculty that evaluates whether a belief, assumption, or self-concept is supported by evidence before it is allowed to shape action.

Extrinsic (Interpersonal): The discernment of readiness in others grounded in evidence, protecting relationships by ensuring trust is extended appropriately.

Integrative (Systemic): The principle that systems remain coherent only when truth-claims are filtered through shared standards before becoming operative.

The ARAA Sequence:

Awareness - When to Use This Symbol

Identify the environmental cues that signal an unchecked assumption:

- Beliefs or self-assessments are being treated as absolute facts without prior examination.
- Individual confidence is being accepted as a substitute for demonstrated competence.
- Social familiarity or personal affinity is being mistaken for legitimate standing or authority.
- Trust is being extended prematurely to unproven claims or withdrawn reactively without cause.

Awareness - When to Use This Symbol (continued)

- High-stakes decisions are being made based on untested assumptions about capacity or intent.

Reflection - Diagnostic Questions

Assess the evidence supporting your current claims or those of others:

- What specific evidence supports this claim beyond simple assertion or confidence?

- What objective criteria am I using to decide whether this person or idea is actually ready?

- Where might social pressure or personal familiarity be bypassing my need for verification?

- What are the potential consequences if this claim is accepted as true without being tested?

Analysis - Failure Modes

Analyze the potential for the distortion of discernment:

Overuse (Cynicism): Treating verification as a tool of distrust; you use impossible epistemic standards to avoid engagement, confusing a skeptical posture with wisdom.

Underuse (Gullibility): Allowing urgency or emotional affinity to override the examination process; you accept unvetted influences because the labor of testing them is too taxing.

Action - Use It Now

Manifest the insight through disciplined behavior:

Identify one belief or assumption currently guiding your decisions, pause to test it against clear evidence or criteria, and confirm its validity before allowing it to inform your next action.

Junior Master of Ceremonies

The Role of Alignment and Contextual Readiness

The Junior Master of Ceremonies manages the Preparing Room, ensuring that the situational framing and prerequisites are correctly established so that examination can occur fairly. This role represents the mental faculty that aligns context and expectations without influencing the final content, ensuring that evaluation reflects truth rather than accident.

The Lenses

Intrinsic (Personal): The mental faculty that aligns internal context and readiness without distorting the truth of a belief or identity before it is tested.

Extrinsic (Interpersonal): The orientation of presence that ensures individuals are situated correctly within a process so their participation is not disadvantaged by confusion.

Integrative (Systemic): *The principle that formation must precede transformation, protecting systems from mistaking situational disorientation for lack of capacity.*

The ARAA Sequence:

Awareness - When to Use This Symbol

Identify the environmental cues that signal a failure of preparation:

- Individuals are being evaluated or judged before they fully understand the procedural context.

- Testing outcomes vary wildly because the situational conditions are inconsistent or unfair.

- Novelty or confusion is interfering with a person's ability to demonstrate their actual readiness.

- Key processes feel arbitrary, rushed, or unclear to those who must participate in them.

Awareness - When to Use This Symbol (continued)

- Simple situational misalignment is being mistaken for a fundamental lack of character or skill.

Reflection - Diagnostic Questions

Assess the conditions under which work or evaluation is occurring:

- Are the external and internal conditions properly aligned for a fair evaluation to occur?

- What prerequisites or preparing steps must be in place before the actual examination begins?

- Where might the current situational misalignment be distorting the final outcome of this work?

- Am I arranging the conditions neutrally, or am I unintentionally influencing the results?

Analysis - Failure Modes

Analyze the potential for the distortion of preparation:

Overuse (Perfectionism): Obsessing over setup to the point of never proceeding to the examination; you use preparation as a form of procrastination.

Underuse (Impetuousness): Rushing into initiation without aligning the conditions; you mistake speed for efficiency, resulting in outcomes that reflect a lack of discipline.

Action - Use It Now

Manifest the insight through disciplined behavior:

Before evaluating a person, idea, or decision, pause to align the context and expectations so the outcome reflects true readiness rather than a failure of preparation.

Pursuivant

The Role of Influence Authentication and Boundary Protection

The Pursuivant guards the lodge against improper external influence, acting as a buffer between the internal order and the uncontrolled environment beyond. This role represents the mental faculty that filters external inputs, pressures, opinions, and incentives, to test their legitimacy before they are allowed to affect judgment.

The Lenses

Intrinsic (Personal): The mental faculty that filters external inputs to distinguish between a legitimate signal and mere environmental noise or pressure.

Extrinsic (Interpersonal): The protection of the threshold that preserves internal coherence and prevents relationships from being shaped by unexamined external forces.

Integrative (Systemic): The principle that integrity depends on disciplined boundaries, ensuring that influence is admitted only by intentional choice.

The ARAA Sequence:

Awareness - When to Use This Symbol

Identify the environmental cues that signal a compromised boundary:

- External pressure is overriding internal judgment and forcing a specific outcome.
- The sheer urgency of a request is being used as a substitute for its actual legitimacy.
- Attention is being repeatedly hijacked by distractions that have no standing in the current work.
- Key decisions feel reactive to outside forces rather than governed by internal purpose.

Awareness - When to Use This Symbol (continued)

- Boundaries have blurred to the point that internal purpose is indistinguishable from external demand.

Reflection - Diagnostic Questions

Assess the legitimacy of the forces currently influencing you:

- Does this specific external influence actually have legitimate standing to be here?

- What criteria am I using to determine whether this input should be admitted or excluded?

- Where am I allowing the volume of an external demand to bypass my process of authentication?

- What external forces are shaping this decision implicitly without my conscious consent?

Analysis - Failure Modes

Analyze the potential for the distortion of authentication:

Overuse (Hyper-Vigilance): Over-fortifying boundaries to the point of total isolation; you treat every external input as a threat to avoid engagement that might change you.

Underuse (Porousness): Confusing openness with a lack of boundaries; you allow any passing emotion or external incentive to dictate your priorities.

Action - Use It Now

Manifest the insight through disciplined behavior:

Notice one external pressure currently influencing your decisions, pause to assess whether it deserves standing, and filter it out if it disrupts your internal coherence.

Tyler

The Role of Attention Gating

The Tyler is stationed outside the lodge to decide whether a potential entrant or disturbance warrants attention at all, alerting the lodge only when engagement is required. This role represents the first line of defense in the mental workshop: the faculty that decides which stimuli are allowed to enter awareness before any further processing occurs.

The Lenses

Intrinsic (Personal): The mental faculty that decides what stimuli, thoughts, or demands are allowed to enter awareness in the first place.

Extrinsic (Interpersonal): The filtering of social and environmental influence at the point of entry to protect presence and prevent relationships from being shaped by every passing demand.

Integrative (Systemic): The principle that boundaries begin with attention; a system cannot govern itself if it cannot control what it chooses to attend to.

The ARAA Sequence:

Awareness - When to Use This Symbol

Identify the environmental cues that signal fragmented attention:

- Attention feels constantly hijacked or fragmented by non-essential stimuli.
- Urgent external stimuli repeatedly override your intentional focus.
- Engagement with a request or distraction feels compulsory rather than a choice.
- External demands dictate your internal priorities by default.

Awareness - When to Use This Symbol (continued)

- Meaningful reflection or sustained work is being repeatedly interrupted.

Reflection - Diagnostic Questions

Assess the gateway of your current awareness:

- Does this specific stimulus or request actually require my attention right now?

- What are the real consequences if this is ignored or deferred for a later time?

- What is currently consuming my attention by default rather than by design?

- Where am I reacting to a knock on the door instead of choosing my engagement?

Analysis - Failure Modes

Analyze the potential for the distortion of focus:

Overuse (Vigilance/Anxiety): Treating every minor stimulus as a threat or urgent call to action; you are so hyper-focused on guarding the door that you never actually enter the lodge to do the Work.

Underuse (Distraction): Allowing constant interruptions to erode your focus; you treat every knock as equally urgent, effectively abandoning your post to the loudest noise.

Action - Use It Now

Manifest the insight through disciplined behavior:

For the next hour, notice what attempts to claim your attention; consciously choose which stimuli to engage and which to exclude, and observe the effect on your clarity.

Guide

The Role of Mentored Passage

The Guide accompanies individuals through unfamiliar or formative experiences, providing the instruction and context required to navigate transitions that would otherwise be overwhelming. This role represents the mental faculty that offers self-support and patience during periods of growth, ensuring that movement through difficulty does not lead to fear or isolation.

The Lenses

Intrinsic (Personal): The mental faculty that offers internal self-support and contextual framing during periods of uncertainty or personal change.

Extrinsic (Interpersonal): The relational act of accompaniment, walking alongside another to provide a stabilizing presence that enables learning through exposure.

Integrative (Systemic): The principle that transformation occurs through guided passage rather than abrupt, uncontextualized change.

The ARAA Sequence:

Awareness - When to Use This Symbol

Identify the environmental cues that signal a need for support:

- Individuals (or parts of yourself) face unfamiliar or destabilizing transitions.
- High anxiety interferes with the ability to engage with a new process or learn.
- Necessary knowledge exists but feels inaccessible because of a lack of support.
- People withdraw when challenged rather than growing from the experience.

**Awareness - When to Use This Symbol
(continued)**

- Personal development feels isolating
  and overwhelming rather than a
  shared journey.

Reflection - Diagnostic Questions

Assess the quality of support and direction being provided:

- What specific support or context would help make this
  transition navigable right now?

- Where might a simple explanation reduce the amount of
  unnecessary fear in this situation?

- How can I offer guidance to myself or others without
  removing their personal agency?

- What pace of accompaniment is appropriate for the
  current level of readiness?

Analysis - Failure Modes

Analyze the potential for the distortion of mentorship:

*Overuse (Enabling): Substituting reassurance for
growth and removing the very challenges required for
transformation; you protect the worker so much they never
develop their own strength.*

*Underuse (Trial by Ordeal): Withholding guidance or
context out of a belief that struggle is the only teacher; you
lose participants to unnecessary friction because you refuse
to provide a stabilizing presence.*

Action - Use It Now

Manifest the insight through disciplined behavior:

When you (or someone else) encounter unfamiliar terrain,
offer a steady presence and a contextual explanation rather
than immediate evaluation or correction.

Tools

Tools are the operative implements that regulate conduct and surface insight. They are used to investigate a situation through disciplined technique squaring an action, circumscribing a desire, or structuring the allocation of effort. They also include indicators of distortion, such as base metals or valuables, which reveal internal attachments and misalignments.

24-Inch Gauge

The Instrument of Intentional Apportionment

The 24-Inch Gauge is a tool used to measure and divide material accurately, providing a fixed standard for consistency and proportion. Speculatively, it is tied to the division of the twenty-four hours of the day, serving as a reminder that time is finite and must be divided deliberately.

The Lenses

Intrinsic (Personal): The mental faculty that allocates attention and effort across competing demands in accordance with purpose rather than impulse.

Extrinsic (Interpersonal): The establishment of expectational clarity by aligning promises and availability with actual, realistic time constraints.

Integrative (Systemic): The principle that time expresses purpose through proportion, revealing what a system truly values by how it distributes its hours.

The ARAA Sequence:

Awareness - When to Use This Symbol

Identify the environmental cues that signal poor apportionment of time:

- Time feels constantly scarce despite significant effort.
- Total commitments routinely exceed the number of available hours.
- Urgent but non-essential tasks consistently crowd out important ones.
- Your availability to others is unclear, inconsistent, or erratic.
- Physical or mental fatigue accumulates due to poor pacing.

Reflection - Diagnostic Questions

Assess your current allocation of finite resources:

- How is my time actually being divided among my various obligations right now?

- Does this specific allocation reflect my stated priorities and values?

- Where am I currently over-committed or significantly under-invested?

- What specific time boundaries need to be clarified to myself or to others?

Analysis - Failure Modes

Analyze the potential for the distortion of time management:

Overuse (Rigidity): Treating the schedule as a weapon of control rather than a tool for proportion; you over-allocate future time to satisfy present ego-demands, creating a brittle structure.

Underuse (Drift): Allowing habit and the loudest demand to dictate your allocation of effort; you confuse being busy with being effective.

Action - Use It Now

Manifest the insight through disciplined behavior:

Review the next twenty-four hours and intentionally apportion time among effort, rest, and obligation; adjust one commitment to better reflect your realistic capacity.

Gavel

The Instrument of Decisive Subtraction

The Gavel is an instrument of subtraction used to break away rough or unnecessary portions of stone so that the material may be fitted for use. It does not shape with precision but clears away friction and excess material so that refinement and development can eventually proceed.

The Lenses

Intrinsic (Personal): The mental faculty that identifies and discards what is counterproductive, excessive, or misaligned with one's core purpose.

Extrinsic (Interpersonal): The clearing of relational friction by removing behaviors or patterns that create repeated conflict or inefficiency in shared effort.

Integrative (Systemic): The principle that emergence requires subtraction, creating space for better forms by removing what obstructs the system's function.

The ARAA Sequence:

Awareness - When to Use This Symbol

Identify the environmental cues that signal a need for removal:

- Progress is blocked by recurring, known obstacles that you have failed to address.
- Ineffective habits persist in your daily routine despite your awareness of them.
- Systemic complexity is growing without providing any corresponding benefit.
- Conflict repeats in your relationships due to specific, unchanged behaviors.
- Total effort increases while the actual results of that effort remain stagnant.

Reflection - Diagnostic Questions

Assess what is obstructing your progress:

- What specific behavior or practice is actively obstructing my progress right now?

- What can be decisively removed from this situation rather than simply managed?

- Where am I tolerating friction out of habit, comfort, or a fear of change?

- What new space or clarity would be created by the act of decisive removal?

Analysis - Failure Modes

Analyze the potential for the distortion of subtraction:

Overuse (Recklessness): Removing material without regard for the underlying structure or consequences; you use subtraction as a form of harshness or punishment.

Underuse (Indulgence): Avoiding decisive action to preserve your own comfort; you continue to carry excess material that you know is an obstruction.

Action - Use It Now

Manifest the insight through disciplined behavior:

Identify one small but persistent behavior or practice that undermines your effectiveness and remove it deliberately; observe what clarity emerges in its absence.

Plumb

The Instrument of Vertical Grounding

The Plumb establishes a true vertical reference line aligned with gravity, allowing a structure to rise upright rather than leaning. It establishes whether a man is standing from a solid foundation or leaning under the influence of external pressures, preferences, or situational drift.

The Lenses

Intrinsic (Personal): The mental faculty that anchors judgment and action to stable principles rather than pressure, preference, or momentary drift.

Extrinsic (Interpersonal): The embodiment of relational dignity that communicates reliability and steadiness to others without dominance or withdrawal.

Integrative (Systemic): The principle that integrity requires a non-negotiable reference point to maintain structural alignment despite external environmental forces.

The ARAA Sequence:

Awareness - When to Use This Symbol

Identify the environmental cues that signal a lack of grounding:

- Your behavior shifts to accommodate external pressure rather than core principles.
- Decisions feel increasingly reactive, opportunistic, or based on immediate convenience.
- Your integrity is being negotiated incrementally in small, seemingly minor ways.
- External incentives or social pressures are starting to distort your judgment.
- Self-respect is eroding through a series of small, unexamined compromises.

Reflection - Diagnostic Questions

Assess your current alignment to your stable reference points:

- What core principle am I actually grounding this specific action in?
- Where am I currently leaning under influence rather than standing upright?
- What specific pressure is currently pulling me off my vertical reference line?
- What would a truly grounded, principled action look like in this situation?

Analysis - Failure Modes

Analyze the potential for the distortion of uprightness:

Overuse (Rigidity): Using uprightness as a weapon of moralism; you confuse being grounded with being inflexible or lacking in compassion.

Underuse (Malleability): Abandoning your reference point for short-term advantage or social harmony; you lean into whichever direction the wind blows.

Action - Use It Now

Manifest the insight through disciplined behavior:

In a situation where pressure is present, pause and identify the principle that should ground your response; act from that reference rather than from impulse.

Level

The Instrument of Horizontal Equanimity

The Level is used to ensure that surfaces are horizontally true, establishing a shared plane so that loads are distributed fairly across a structure. It ensures shared ground and balance, preventing proximity, emotion, or recency from distorting one's assessment of a situation.

The Lenses

Intrinsic (Personal): The mental faculty that moderates internal bias and establishes an equitable perspective before comparison or cooperation proceeds.

Extrinsic (Interpersonal): The establishment of shared ground that enables cooperation without resentment and disagreement without domination.

Integrative (Systemic): The principle of equanimity that requires a temporal perspective, preventing the system from overcorrecting for momentary discomfort.

The ARAA Sequence:

Awareness - When to Use This Symbol

Identify the environmental cues that signal an imbalance of footing or perspective:

- Situations feel fundamentally unfair or skewed without a clear, underlying pattern.
- Short-term discomfort is being mistaken for a permanent structural injustice.
- Long-term inequities are being normalized, overlooked, or ignored over time.
- Emotional proximity to a person or event is distorting your assessment of fairness.

**Awareness - When to Use This Symbol
(continued)**

- Your reactions to a situation are
  clearly disproportionate to the actual
  imbalance present.

Reflection - Diagnostic Questions

Assess the balance of the conditions you are currently working
within:

- Are the current conditions actually balanced for
  everyone involved in this interaction?

- Is this a temporary deviation from the norm, or is it a
  persistent, structural imbalance?

- Over the span of a lifetime, does this specific issue
  represent a minor bump or a mountain?

- What specific adjustment would restore a sense of
  shared ground proportionally?

Analysis - Failure Modes

Analyze the potential for the distortion of equality:

*Overuse (Forced Equality): Confusing fairness with
immediate comfort or forced sameness; you overcorrect for
every minor deviation, stifling necessary growth.*

*Underuse (Myopia): Ignoring gradual inequities because
they feel normal in the short term; you fail to apply a wider
temporal horizon to your judgments.*

Action - Use It Now

Manifest the insight through disciplined behavior:

When a situation feels destabilizing, extend your time
horizon; assess whether the imbalance is momentary or
structural and respond with proportion.

Square

The Instrument of Ethical Validation

The Square is used to test whether angles are true and surfaces meet correctly, ensuring that work conforms to established standards. It verifies the rightness of an action, asking whether it is rightly formed according to principle rather than convenience or rationalization.

The Lenses

Intrinsic (Personal): The mental faculty that tests actions and judgments against established principles rather than pressure or preference.

Extrinsic (Interpersonal): The maintenance of ethical fairness that ensures relationships are governed by predictability and trust rather than favoritism.

Integrative (Systemic): The principle of moral epistemology; the requirement that rightness must be knowable, testable, and explicitly defined.

The ARAA Sequence:

Awareness - When to Use This Symbol

Identify the environmental cues that signal a lack of ethical alignment:

- Decisions are being justified by emotional vibe rather than by principled reasoning.
- Standards of conduct are being invoked inconsistently depending on who is involved.
- Actions are being defended after the fact instead of being validated before they were taken.
- Fairness feels arbitrary or selective based on the specific situation or personal affinity.

- Accountability is being avoided through the use of ambiguity or vague language.

Reflection - Diagnostic Questions

Assess the squareness of your current or intended actions:

- What specific moral or professional standard am I using to judge this action?

- Does this intended action actually meet that standard before it is taken?

- Where might my personal convenience be overriding my commitment to correctness?

- Can this specific decision be explained and defended coherently to a neutral observer?

Analysis - Failure Modes

Analyze the potential for the distortion of standards:

Overuse (Legalism): Treating standards as rigid weapons to judge others while ignoring the spirit of the law; using the Square to assert moral superiority.

Underuse (Malleability): Treating standards as flexible tools that can be bent to suit your preference or to avoid social friction; resulting in a work that cannot hold weight.

Action - Use It Now

Manifest the insight through disciplined behavior:

Before taking a consequential action, explicitly state the principle it must meet, then test the action against that principle before you proceed.

Trowel

The Instrument of Calibrated Cohesion

The Trowel is used to spread mortar and bind individual stones together into a unified structure. Symbolically, it represents the application of calibrated care and empathy, sufficient to connect and unify a group, but not so much as to overwhelm the structure or autonomy of the parts.

The Lenses

Intrinsic (Personal): The mental faculty that applies care and attention in a measured way, sufficient to connect, but respecting of internal boundaries.

Extrinsic (Interpersonal): The deliberate cultivation of cohesion within a group, ensuring that relationships and projects cohere rather than fragment.

Integrative (Systemic): The principle that community is built through ongoing effort; cohesion does not arise automatically but through intentional binding.

The ARAA Sequence:

Awareness - When to Use This Symbol

Identify the environmental cues that signal a loss of cohesion:

- Groups are beginning to fragment into silos despite having a shared purpose.
- Relationships are weakening through simple neglect rather than through active conflict.
- Collaboration feels brittle, transactional, or lacks a sense of shared investment.
- Small gaps in communication or care are starting to undermine larger structures.
- Cohesion is being assumed as a given, but it is not being actively enacted or maintained.

Reflection - Diagnostic Questions

Assess the quality of the mortar in your current relationships:

- Where is the cohesion in this specific relationship or project currently weakening?

- What specific kind of care or attention would strengthen the connection right now?

- Am I currently under-applying care through neglect, or over-applying it through smothering?

- What must be bound together here without altering the underlying structure or roles?

Analysis - Failure Modes

Analyze the potential for the distortion of care:

Overuse (Smothering): Confusing care with indulgence; you spread mortar over cracks that need to be chiseled out, using kindness to avoid necessary friction.

Underuse (Neglect): Assuming that cohesion will maintain itself without effort; you leave your connections dry-stacked and vulnerable to collapse under strain.

Action - Use It Now

Manifest the insight through disciplined behavior:

Identify one relationship or collaboration showing early signs of strain; apply a small, deliberate act of care to strengthen cohesion without altering expectations.

Compasses

The Instrument of Containment through Proportion

The Compasses are used to draw circles, set bounds, and establish proportion. Speculatively, they represent the faculty of self-restraint, defining the limits within which form is created and impulse is circumscribed so that desire does not exceed capacity or principle.

The Lenses

Intrinsic (Personal): The mental faculty that circumscribes desire and ambition so that impulse is shaped into a workable and sustainable form.

Extrinsic (Interpersonal): The establishment of boundary dignity, ensuring relationships remain respectful and safe by preventing unchecked expectation or overreach.

Integrative (Systemic): The principle that growth must be shaped by proportion to remain constructive, preventing systems from collapsing under their own unmanaged expansion.

The ARAA Sequence:

Awareness - When to Use This Symbol

Identify the environmental cues that signal a lack of restraint or defined limits:

- Personal desire or ambition has begun to exceed your available capacity or resources.
- Actions are being driven by a need for expansion without regard for long-term consequences.
- Relational or professional boundaries are unclear or are being routinely crossed.
- Rapid growth or expansion is creating instability rather than healthy development.

Awareness - When to Use This Symbol (continued)

- Restraint is being viewed as an unnecessary limitation rather than a necessary discipline.

Reflection - Diagnostic Questions

Assess the boundaries and proportions of your current impulses:

- What specific boundary must be set in this situation for it to remain healthy?

- Where has my current desire or ambition exceeded the bounds of proportion?

- What is the likely outcome if this current impulse continues to grow unchecked?

- How can a deliberate act of restraint preserve my long-term intentions?

Analysis - Failure Modes

Analyze the potential for the distortion of limits:

Overuse (Suppression): Over-constraining yourself or others to the point of stifling legitimate growth; using boundaries to avoid the risks of engagement.

Underuse (Self-Indulgence): Allowing desire to define your limits rather than your principles; setting boundaries only reactively after harm has occurred.

Action - Use It Now

Manifest the insight through disciplined behavior:

Identify one desire or ambition currently influencing your decisions; set a clear, proportionate boundary that allows progress without excess, and commit to honoring it.

Hoodwink

The Instrument of Intentional Suspension

The Hoodwink is a tool used to temporarily obscure sight, preventing visual perception so that an individual must rely on guidance and internal senses. It is not an instrument of deception, but of preparation, used to withhold premature perception and bracket assumptions so that new understanding can form without distortion.

The Lenses

Intrinsic (Personal): The mental faculty that brackets assumptions and habitual interpretations so that experience can unfold without immediate categorization.

Extrinsic (Interpersonal): The embodiment of humility in perception, acknowledging the limits of one's viewpoint to enable trust and receptivity in relationships.

Integrative (Systemic): The principle of epistemic openness, where systems permit the temporary suspension of certainty to prevent premature closure and allow for adaptation.

The ARAA Sequence:

Awareness - When to Use This Symbol

Identify the environmental cues that signal a need to suspend judgment:

- Certainty regarding an outcome or a person is preceding the actual evidence.
- Your interpretation of an event is hardening too quickly before all facts are known.
- Habitual assumptions are dominating your perception of a new experience.
- A disagreement is escalating into defensiveness because you believe you already see the truth.

Awareness - When to Use This Symbol (continued)

- Learning has stalled because you feel overconfident in your existing knowledge.

Reflection - Diagnostic Questions

Assess your willingness to enter a state of temporary not-knowing:

- What specific assumptions am I carrying into this situation right now?

- What would change in my perspective if I suspended my judgment temporarily?

- Where might my current certainty be obstructing a deeper understanding of the situation?

- What can I observe in this moment if I stop trying to explain or categorize it?

Analysis - Failure Modes

Analyze the potential for the distortion of unknowing:

Overuse (Paralysis): Treating the suspension of judgment as an excuse for permanent indecision; using unknowing to avoid the friction of making a choice.

Underuse (Premature Closure): Refusing to wear the Hoodwink at the threshold of a new experience; insisting on seeing everything on your own terms immediately.

Action - Use It Now

Manifest the insight through disciplined behavior:

In a situation where you feel certain, pause and deliberately suspend judgment; observe what becomes visible when you allow not-knowing to precede your conclusion.

Entered Apprentice

The Perspective of the Disciplined Beginner

The Entered Apprentice represents the beginning of intentional development under guidance, marking the transition from self-directed assumptions to disciplined learning. The role exists to establish foundations by cultivating attention, receptivity, and trust in the instructional structure.

The Lenses

Intrinsic (Personal): The intentional act of beginning, prioritized by learning over performance and the restraint of premature certainty.

Extrinsic (Interpersonal): The establishment of an instructional relationship where guidance is received as support rather than as a threat to one's ego.

Integrative (Systemic): The principle that development begins with intentional unknowing, creating the internal space required for genuine transformation.

The ARAA Sequence:

Awareness - When to Use This Symbol

Identify the environmental cues that signal a resistance to the beginning:

- You feel a resistance to instruction despite lacking demonstrated competence in a new area.
- Your learning process feels rushed, fragmented, or purely superficial.
- Constructive feedback is being interpreted as personal criticism rather than as necessary guidance.
- You find yourself seeking recognition or status before you have achieved basic mastery.

Awareness - When to Use This Symbol (continued)

- The foundations of a project or habit feel shaky because the beginner's stage was bypassed.

Reflection - Diagnostic Questions

Assess your current posture as a learner:

- What am I being asked to learn or observe before I am permitted to act or lead?

- Where am I currently resisting guidance out of a sense of impatience or pride?

- Have I truly understood the basic foundations of this work before trying to move forward?

- Am I prioritizing the appearance of competence over the actual labor of learning?

Analysis - Failure Modes

Analyze the potential for the distortion of the apprentice phase:

Overuse (Passivity): Using the Apprentice label to avoid taking necessary responsibility; turning learning into a permanent state of stalling to escape the friction of labor.

Underuse (Premature Certainty): Attempting to lead, critique, or innovate before you have understood the basic grammar of the situation; treating foundations as hurdles to be cleared rather than resources to be integrated.

Action - Use It Now

Manifest the insight through disciplined behavior:

Choose one area where you believe you already know how this works. For the next interaction, deliberately set aside that assumption and approach it as if encountering it for the first time.

Fellowcraft

The Perspective of Development Through Structured Effort

The Fellowcraft represents the phase of development where learned skills are applied through practice, collaboration, and increasing responsibility under established standards. This role transforms initial understanding into actual capability through disciplined repetition and engagement with the work.

The Lenses

Intrinsic (Personal): The intentional development of skill through sustained effort, attention to detail, and the willingness to revise one's approach based on evidence.

Extrinsic (Interpersonal): The engagement in reciprocal exchange, where knowledge flows between peers and mentors through constructive feedback and shared standards.

Integrative (Systemic): The principle that capability emerges through structure applied over time, embedding growth within repeatable, measurable processes.

The ARAA Sequence:

Awareness - When to Use This Symbol

Identify the environmental cues that signal a stagnation in development:

- Skill acquisition feels inconsistent, unmeasured, or lacks a clear trajectory of improvement.
- You are expending high levels of effort, but your actual improvement over time is unclear.
- Professional or personal feedback is absent, being ignored, or is being taken too personally to be useful.
- Collaboration with others produces interpersonal friction rather than collective learning.

Awareness - When to Use This Symbol (continued)

- Standards for the work exist but are being applied unevenly or haphazardly.

Reflection - Diagnostic Questions

Assess the quality and structure of your current efforts:

- What specific skill or responsibility am I actively practicing and refining right now?

- How am I specifically measuring my improvement in this area over time?

- Where am I actively exchanging feedback with others rather than working in isolation?

- What explicit standards am I using to evaluate my own progress and readiness?

Analysis - Failure Modes

Analyze the potential for the distortion of the development phase:

Overuse (Competition): Prioritizing individual recognition over coordinated success; using emerging competence to distance yourself from peers rather than to support the whole.

Underuse (Stagnation): Confusing busy-ness with actual development; repeating the same actions without a commitment to refinement or an integration of feedback.

Action - Use It Now

Manifest the insight through disciplined behavior:

Select one skill you are currently developing; define a clear standard for improvement and invite specific feedback after your next attempt, then adjust your approach.

Master Mason

The Perspective of Agency and Stewardship

The Master Mason represents the transition from development to agency, assuming full accountability for direction, consequences, and the impact of decisions on the whole system. This role is defined by the capacity to take responsibility for the final judgment and the stewardship of others.

The Lenses

Intrinsic (Personal): The capacity to take responsibility for direction and the consequences of one's actions rather than merely contributing effort.

Extrinsic (Interpersonal): The stewardship of influence, where authority is exercised with consideration for its effects on the behavior, morale, and trust of others.

Integrative (Systemic): The principle that agency shapes systems; decisions made at this level rippling outward to influence the long-term durability of the whole.

The ARAA Sequence:

Awareness - When to Use This Symbol

Identify the environmental cues that signal a failure of agency or stewardship:

- Important decisions are being delayed or avoided due to a fear of the potential consequences.
- Responsibility for outcomes is diffuse, unclear, or is being repeatedly deferred to others.
- Authority exists in name or title but is not being manifested in actual practice or direction.
- The final outcomes of a project suffer despite the team having sufficient skill and effort.

Awareness - When to Use This Symbol (continued)

- The direction of the work changes frequently without a clear or communicated rationale.

Reflection - Diagnostic Questions

Assess your current level of responsibility and direction:

- Where am I currently avoiding direction by seeking more information or unnecessary permission?

- What specific outcomes am I ultimately responsible for in this moment?

- How does my current direction, or lack of it, influence others' ability to act effectively?

- Where do I need to own the consequences of a decision rather than delegating them away?

Analysis - Failure Modes

Analyze the potential for the distortion of agency:

Overuse (Control): Confusing direction with micromanagement; acting decisively but without regard for the impact on others, using agency to dominate rather than steward.

Underuse (Abdication): Deferring responsibility or over-consulting to avoid the weight of final judgment; leaving the system to fracture under unowned authority.

Action - Use It Now

Manifest the insight through disciplined behavior:

Identify one decision you have been postponing due to uncertainty; choose a direction, communicate it clearly, and commit to adjusting responsibly based on the results.

Cabletow

The Instrument of Calibrated Commitment

The Cabletow is a tool used operatively as a rope or line to signify connection and constraint. Its length defines a measurable tether that is neither infinite nor rigid, representing the honest calibration of moral and social obligation against an individual's actual capacity.

The Lenses

Intrinsic (Personal): The mental faculty that evaluates whether a commitment fits within available resources, resilience, and personal context.

Extrinsic (Interpersonal): The maintenance of proportionate tension in relationships, ensuring that commitments remain sustainable rather than heroic but brittle.

Integrative (Systemic): The principle that freedom depends on proportionate obligation, ensuring that commitments support agency rather than destroying it through overextension.

The ARAA Sequence:

Awareness - When to Use This Symbol

Identify the environmental cues that signal a lack of calibrated commitment:

- Commitments are accumulating significantly faster than your actual capacity to fulfill them.
- A Yes is offered reflexively to requests and then regretted almost immediately afterward.
- Personal guilt is being used as a substitute for an honest assessment of your abilities.
- Burnout follows intense periods of overextension where you ignored your own limits.

Awareness - When to Use This Symbol (continued)

- Responsibility begins to feel coercive or burdensome rather than a chosen duty.

Reflection - Diagnostic Questions

Assess the length and tension of your current obligations:

- What is my actual, honest capacity for new commitments right now?

- Does this specific obligation fit within my present capacity without causing harm?

- What are the likely consequences to myself and others if I accept more than I can sustain?

- Where might personal honesty require a renegotiation of an existing commitment?

Analysis - Failure Modes

Analyze the potential for the distortion of obligation:

Overuse (Martyrdom): Confusing overextension with virtue; you treat the Cabletow as if it were infinitely elastic until you suffer a brittle breakdown.

Underuse (Avoidance): Using capacity as an excuse to avoid legitimate responsibility or growth; you keep your tether so short you never build strength.

Action - Use It Now

Manifest the insight through disciplined behavior:

Review one current commitment; assess whether it fits your present capacity and adjust by recommitting, renegotiating, or releasing, to align ability with obligation.

Three Knocks

The Instrument of Committed Initiation

The Three Knocks function as a formal signal indicating presence, intention, and a willingness to be examined at a guarded threshold. They represent the grammar of transformation, moving an individual from mere curiosity to named intention and, finally, to a committed request for engagement.

The Lenses

Intrinsic (Personal): The mental faculty that converts vague desire into specific intention and, finally, into committed, outward action.

Extrinsic (Interpersonal): The relational act of invitation and acknowledgment, where a request for entry is made with respect for the responder's discernment.

Integrative (Systemic): The principle that development requires conscious entry points and thresholds to distinguish desire from true readiness.

The ARAA Sequence:

Awareness - When to Use This Symbol

Identify the environmental cues that signal a need for intentional entry:

- A desire for change is present in your mind, but a concrete commitment to that change is absent.

- Transitions in your life are being entered passively or accidentally rather than intentionally.

- Your engagement with a process remains tentative, half-hearted, or easily reversible.

- You find yourself expecting outcomes without being willing to submit to the required process.

Awareness - When to Use This Symbol (continued)

- Important thresholds in your work or relationships feel blurred, bypassed, or ignored.

Reflection - Diagnostic Questions

Assess your readiness to commit to a new threshold:

- What specific threshold am I approaching in my life or work right now?

- Have I moved beyond mere seeking into named intention and committed action?

- Am I truly willing to be examined and changed as part of this transition?

- What specific response or requirement am I prepared to receive from the other side?

Analysis - Failure Modes

Analyze the potential for the distortion of entry:

Overuse (Coercion): Using the Knock to force a response or demand entry based on entitlement; you try to bypass examination by knocking louder rather than becoming readier.

Underuse (Passivity): Remaining in a state of perpetual seeking without ever naming your desire; waiting for the world to initiate your development for you.

Action - Use It Now

Manifest the insight through disciplined behavior:

Identify one area where you want change but have not yet committed; name your intention clearly and acknowledge the examination or response that must follow.

Left Slipper

The Instrument of Intentional Pledge

The Left Slipper is a tool associated with a formal change in posture at a threshold, signifying the moment a promise is made and obligation is accepted. It represents the declared intention to be bound to a commitment, even before the results of that commitment exist.

The Lenses

Intrinsic (Personal): The mental faculty that affirms intent and accepts future accountability before any results are manifest.

Extrinsic (Interpersonal): The signaling of a known agreement that allows others to orient their expectations and begin forming trust based on stated intent.

Integrative (Systemic): The principle that identity begins forming the moment a chosen obligation is explicitly accepted.

The ARAA Sequence:

Awareness - When to Use This Symbol

Identify the environmental cues that signal uncommitted participation:

- You are participating in a project or group without having made an explicit, stated commitment.

- Your promises to others remain vague, hedged, or intentionally non-committal.

- You feel an internal resistance to being held accountable at the entry point of a task.

- Trust in a relationship is being delayed because your actual intent remains unclear to the other party.

Awareness - When to Use This Symbol (continued)

- You are reaping the benefits of a system without formally accepting its burdens.

Reflection - Diagnostic Questions

Assess the clarity of your current pledges:

- What specific obligation am I explicitly accepting in this situation?

- Do I fully understand what this promise will require of my time and integrity?

- What reasonable expectations will others form based on this pledge?

- Am I truly consenting to be evaluated by my future performance?

Analysis - Failure Modes

Analyze the potential for the distortion of promising:

Overuse (Performative Pledging): Making promises to gain immediate status or approval without any actual intention of following through; treating the pledge as a mere gesture.

Underuse (Ambiguity): Resisting a clear promise to remain flexible and uncommitted; avoiding accountability by keeping your intent implied rather than stated.

Action - Use It Now

Manifest the insight through disciplined behavior:

Before entering a new responsibility, state the promise clearly; including exactly what you are committing to and what you are not.

Right Slipper

The Instrument of Verified Follow-Through

The Right Slipper signifies a promise fulfilled, the visible confirmation that an obligation previously accepted has been carried through to completion. It is the tool of proof rather than pledge, where credibility is established by outcome rather than explanation.

The Lenses

Intrinsic (Personal): The mental faculty that measures one's own integrity by actual results rather than by good intentions.

Extrinsic (Interpersonal): The realization of trust, where repeated follow-through stabilizes expectations and deepens the confidence of others.

Integrative (Systemic): The principle that character is revealed through fulfilled action, allowing for coordination and continuity within a system.

The ARAA Sequence:

Awareness - When to Use This Symbol

Identify the environmental cues that signal a failure of completion:

- Your stated promises currently outnumber your actual, visible results.
- Trust in your reliability is eroding despite your continued good intentions.
- You find yourself habitually deflecting accountability with long explanations or excuses.
- Your identity feels purely aspirational because it is not yet embodied in your actions.

Awareness - When to Use This Symbol (continued)

- Others hesitate to rely on you for high-stakes tasks because your follow-through is inconsistent.

Reflection - Diagnostic Questions

Assess the evidence of your integrity:

- What specific obligation have I actually fulfilled to its completion?

- Where does the final outcome of my work confirm or contradict my original intent?

- What level of trust have I actually earned through my recent actions?

- What does this specific completion reveal about my current reliability?

Analysis - Failure Modes

Analyze the potential for the distortion of follow-through:

Overuse (Outcome Obsession): Completing tasks selectively solely to manage the perception of your reliability; prioritizing the appearance of follow-through over quality.

Underuse (Explanation): Substituting reasons and narratives for actual completion; hoping that your intent will be accepted in place of finished work.

Action - Use It Now

Manifest the insight through disciplined behavior:

Identify one obligation you have already accepted; complete it fully and allow the outcome to speak for itself without further commentary.

Money and Valuables

The Indicator of Instrumental Distortion

Money and Valuables are tools of exchange and measurement that must be set aside in the lodge to distinguish instrumental value from intrinsic worth. They serve as indicators of status distortion, reminding the Mason that metrics and incentives can often blind judgment to deeper principles.

The Lenses

Intrinsic (Personal): The mental faculty that recognizes when personal metrics, incentives, or rewards are distorting internal judgment.

Extrinsic (Interpersonal): The awareness of status distortion that occurs when wealth or display alters power dynamics and biases the perception of worth.

Integrative (Systemic): The principle that systems fail when instrumental exchange logic supplants the intrinsic worth of people or principles.

The ARAA Sequence:

Awareness - When to Use This Symbol

Identify the environmental cues that signal transactional distortion:

- External incentives or rewards are starting to distort your behavior or motivations.
- You are inferring a person's status or authority from their possessions or outward display.
- Monetary or efficiency metrics are beginning to override moral judgment or core principles.
- Your personal or professional relationships are becoming increasingly transactional.

Awareness - When to Use This Symbol (continued)

- You find yourself confusing the price of an effort with its actual worth.

Reflection - Diagnostic Questions

Assess the influence of exchange logic on your current situation:

- What is actually being measured in this situation and why is that being tracked?

- Where might the pursuit of instrumental value be distorting my current judgment?

- What elements of this situation cannot, and should not, be bought or traded?

- How would my approach to this change if all incentives and rewards were removed?

Analysis - Failure Modes

Analyze the potential for the distortion of valuation:

Overuse (Optimization): Attempting to apply exchange logic to every domain of life; treating care and integrity as commodities to be traded.

Underuse (Financial Blindness): Ignoring the reality of instrumental needs under a guise of spirituality; failing to steward the resources required for the work.

Action - Use It Now

Manifest the insight through disciplined behavior:

In a current decision, identify whether incentives are shaping your behavior; ask if the matter requires exchange or discernment.

Mineral & Metallic Substances

The Indicator of Defensive Hardening

Mineral and Metallic Substances represent materials that harden and resist, used for protection but becoming obstructive when over-applied. In the lodge, they symbolize the defensive postures, emotional, cognitive, or identity-based, that must be divested for growth to occur.

The Lenses

Intrinsic (Personal): The mental faculty that recognizes when internal defenses have become rigid and obstructive rather than protective.

Extrinsic (Interpersonal): The dynamic of softening defensive hardening to allow for communication, vulnerability, and trust to resume.

Integrative (Systemic): The principle that systems degrade when defensive structures (outdated roles or assumptions) outlive their original purpose.

The ARAA Sequence:

Awareness - When to Use This Symbol

Identify the environmental cues that signal rigid defensiveness:

- Your internal defensiveness has begun to replace your natural curiosity.
- You perceive constructive criticism as a direct personal threat to your identity.
- Your self-concept has become rigid, performative, or difficult to challenge.
- You find yourself resisting feedback reflexively before you have even processed it.
- Your emotional reactions to others have hardened into a permanent defensive posture.

Reflection - Diagnostic Questions

Assess the state of your internal armor:

- What specific belief or identity am I defending that no longer needs my protection?
- Where has internal hardness replaced my ability to use discernment?
- What armor once served a purpose but now only obstructs my personal growth?
- What elements of my posture could be softened without collapsing my integrity?

Analysis - Failure Modes

Analyze the potential for the distortion of protection:

Overuse (Rigidity): Using defenses to avoid all vulnerability, making yourself un-teachable; mistaking hardness for strength until you become brittle.

Underuse (Discernment-less Vulnerability): Stripping away all protection prematurely in unsafe environments; confusing softness with a total lack of integrity.

Action - Use It Now

Manifest the insight through disciplined behavior:

Notice a situation where you feel defensive; identify what is being protected and assess whether that protection is still necessary or now obstructive.

The Ruffians

The Indicator of Suppression and Corrosion

The Ruffians are forces that suppress, destabilize, and corrode the internal conditions required for meaningful work. They represent universal psychological and environmental mechanisms, Fear, Uncertainty, and Doubt, that restrict the internal liberty necessary for truth, agency, and integrity to function.

The Lenses

Intrinsic (Personal): The recognition of internal suppression where fear inhibits speech, uncertainty limits expression, and doubt erodes conviction.

Extrinsic (Interpersonal): The degradation of trust where dialogue becomes guarded, expression narrows, and disagreement is avoided rather than examined.

Integrative (Systemic): The principle that systems fail when they suppress interior liberty, making integrity unsustainable and replacing the Work with performative compliance.

The ARAA Sequence:

Awareness - When to Use This Symbol

Identify the environmental cues that signal the corrosion of integrity:

- Honest speech feels unsafe or carries an unspoken threat of consequence.
- Your range of expression narrows significantly without any explicit prohibition.
- Decisions stall or feel hollow despite an apparent surface-level agreement.
- Performative compliance has replaced genuine conviction in your actions.

Awareness - When to Use This Symbol (continued)

- Trust is eroding while the formal structure of the relationship or organization remains intact.

Reflection - Diagnostic Questions

Assess the state of your interior liberty:

- Where am I currently remaining silent out of fear rather than out of wisdom or discernment?

- What specific uncertainty is limiting how fully I can express myself in this situation?

- What specific doubt is currently eroding my internal clarity or conviction?

- Which freedom, speech, expression, or thought, has been compromised first in this environment?

Analysis - Failure Modes

Analyze the potential for the distortion of resistance:

Overuse (Hyper-Antagonism): Treating every moment of necessary caution or social tact as a Ruffian attack; destroying the very conditions you claim to protect.

Underuse (Compliance): Mistaking silence and submission for peace or alignment; allowing your integrity to be struck away until you are a Mason in name only.

Action - Use It Now

Manifest the insight through disciplined behavior:

Notice a situation where progress feels stalled or hollow; identify whether fear, uncertainty, or doubt is most active and name one condition that would restore truthful speech.

The Volume of Sacred Law

The Foundation of Alignment to Enduring Principle

The Volume of Sacred Law (VSL) is the stable point of reference that precedes personal opinion or situational pressure. It provides the moral orientation necessary for obligations to be grounded in principles that endure beyond individual preference, convenience, or circumstance.

The Lenses

Intrinsic (Personal): The mental faculty that orients thought and action toward values that endure beyond impulse, appetite, or momentary context.

Extrinsic (Interpersonal): The establishment of shared meaning that allows for cooperation without coercion, grounding relationships in a common axis of value.

Integrative (Systemic): The principle that systems require a stable moral orientation to sustain trust, continuity, and legitimacy over time.

The ARAA Sequence:

Awareness - When to Use This Symbol

Identify the environmental cues that signal a loss of moral orientation:

- Your decisions shift frequently based on personal convenience or external pressure.
- Standards of conduct feel negotiable rather than principled when you are under stress.
- Your commitments to others begin to erode as soon as circumstances become difficult.
- Coordination with others fails because of fundamental ambiguity regarding shared values.

Awareness - When to Use This Symbol (continued)

- Meaning is being sought through social consensus rather than through grounded principles.

Reflection - Diagnostic Questions

Assess your alignment with your enduring reference points:

- What specific, enduring principle am I actually aligning this action to right now?

- Would this specific choice remain valid if it were under intense pressure or public scrutiny?

- What reference actually governs my current obligation is it my preference or is it a principle?

- Where has my alignment to values been replaced by a negotiation for convenience?

Analysis - Failure Modes

Analyze the potential for the distortion of alignment:

Overuse (Moralism): Substituting the literal text for the actual principle; using the VSL to suppress dissent or police others rather than to orient your own work.

Underuse (Relativism): Treating all standards as flexible or situational; allowing your orientation to drift until you have no solid ground for an obligation.

Action - Use It Now

Manifest the insight through disciplined behavior:

Before making a consequential decision, identify the principle you are aligning to and test whether your action remains coherent when measured against it.

Systems of Meaning

Systems represent the intellectual structures through which we discover and communicate meaning. Drawing from the liberal arts and sciences, these symbols provide the methods by which clarity emerges, whether through the logic of an argument, the proportion of a design, or the harmony of a relationship.

Grammar

The System for Structuring Meaning

Grammar governs the structure of language, providing the rules by which meaning is formed and preserved. It makes thought intelligible by ordering ideas before persuasion or evaluation occur, ensuring that communication is legible and can be shared reliably.

The Lenses

Intrinsic (Personal): The mental faculty that orders internal thought so ideas can be apprehended and related without confusion.

Extrinsic (Interpersonal): The semantic interplay where shared structure allows multiple parties to coordinate understanding and refine meaning together.

Integrative (Systemic): The principle that order precedes meaning, enabling the continuity of knowledge and culture through stable structures of expression.

The ARAA Sequence:

Awareness - When to Use This Symbol

Identify the environmental cues that signal a lack of structural clarity:

- Ideas feel internally correct but cannot be expressed or written clearly.
- Conversations loop repeatedly due to misunderstood terms or vague definitions.
- Disagreements center more on what was meant than on the actual substance of the issue.
- The meaning of a statement shifts unintentionally in the middle of a discussion.

Awareness - When to Use This Symbol (continued)

- The complexity of an idea overwhelms the ability to comprehend or share it.

Reflection - Diagnostic Questions

Assess the structural integrity of your thoughts and expressions:

- How is this specific idea currently structured in my mind?

- Are my primary terms defined consistently for myself and for others?

- What specific relationships between concepts am I implying in this statement?

- Where might a lack of structure be obscuring the meaning I intend to share?

Analysis - Failure Modes

Analyze the potential for the distortion of structure:

Overuse (Pedantry): Overloading concepts with excessive definition; using structure as a way to dominate a conversation rather than to clarify it.

Underuse (Vagueness): Treating structure as secondary to feeling or vibe; relying on shifting definitions to avoid being pinned down.

Action - Use It Now

Manifest the insight through disciplined behavior:

Take a thought or statement that feels unclear and rewrite it with explicit structure; define terms, clarify relationships, and simplify the form.

Rhetoric

The System for Communal Meaning-Making

Rhetoric governs the effective use of language in relation to an audience, shaping how meaning is framed and delivered. It moves meaning between people by anticipating how words will land and adjusting expression to fit the specific relationship, timing, and circumstance.

The Lenses

Intrinsic (Personal): The mental faculty that anticipates the reception of one's words, adjusting tone and frame to match the context.

Extrinsic (Interpersonal): The narrative stance that positions speaker and listener, inviting cooperation or resistance through the framing of ideas.

Integrative (Systemic): The principle that meaning is a relational effect; ideas influence systems only insofar as they are received and understood.

The ARAA Sequence:

Awareness - When to Use This Symbol

Identify the environmental cues that signal a failure of communication resonance:

- Your messages are technically correct but are consistently poorly received.
- Conflict escalates quickly due to the tone of delivery rather than the actual content.
- Audiences or individuals disengage from you despite your sound reasoning.
- Your attempts at persuasion feel forced, robotic, or manipulative.

Awareness - When to Use This Symbol (continued)

- Your communication repeatedly misses the emotional or situational context of the moment.

Reflection - Diagnostic Questions

Assess the relational impact of your communication:

- Who am I actually speaking to right now, and what do they specifically need to hear?

- How might this specific message land given the current timing and context?

- What stance does my language create, is it inviting or is it alienating?

- Am I seeking genuine communion and understanding, or am I just seeking compliance?

Analysis - Failure Modes

Analyze the potential for the distortion of influence:

Overuse (Manipulation): Prioritizing the effect of words over their integrity; using emotional framing to bypass another's understanding.

Underuse (Abrasiveness): Ignoring the relational context and assuming the truth should be enough; confusing bluntness with honesty.

Action - Use It Now

Manifest the insight through disciplined behavior:

Before speaking or writing, pause to consider the audience and context; adjust your framing so the meaning can be shared without distortion.

Logic

The System for Testing Coherence

Logic governs the rules of valid reasoning, providing the methods to test whether conclusions follow from premises and whether arguments cohere. It determines whether a claim can be justified independently of how it is expressed or how well it is received.

The Lenses

Intrinsic (Personal): The mental faculty that checks internal reasoning for contradictions, fallacies, or unsupported leaps in thought.

Extrinsic (Interpersonal): The reasoned coherence that provides a neutral ground where claims can be evaluated independently of status or sentiment.

Integrative (Systemic): The principle that validity constrains belief and action, providing an invisible architecture that supports trust and predictability.

The ARAA Sequence:

Awareness - When to Use This Symbol

Identify the environmental cues that signal a failure of reasoning:

- Your conclusions feel convincing but lack any visible supporting evidence.
- Arguments (yours or others') shift premises in the middle of a discussion.
- Internal or external contradictions are being ignored or rationalized away.
- Personal authority is being used as a substitute for sound, step-by-step reasoning.

Awareness - When to Use This Symbol (continued)

- Disagreements center on what follows from what rather than on the facts themselves.

Reflection - Diagnostic Questions

Assess the validity of your current reasoning:

- What specific premises am I actually relying on to reach this conclusion?

- Does this specific conclusion follow necessarily, or is it merely probabilistic?

- Where might a contradiction be present in my current argument or belief?

- What specific piece of evidence would falsify this claim if it were found?

Analysis - Failure Modes

Analyze the potential for the distortion of reasoning:

Overuse (Rationalism): Treating logical consistency as the only proof of truth; ignoring empirical evidence or human context that doesn't fit a syllogism.

Underuse (Emotionalism): Allowing consistency to be overwritten by however you feel; moving the goalposts of reasoning to defend a current mood.

Action - Use It Now

Manifest the insight through disciplined behavior:

Take a claim you currently accept; list its premises and trace the inference step by step to verify that the conclusion actually follows.

Arithmetic

The System for Quantifying Reality

Arithmetic governs the use of number to count, compare, and calculate, rendering quantity and proportion explicit. It allows for magnitude, frequency, and trends to be made intelligible, ensuring that processes can be repeated with consistency and results can be tracked.

The Lenses

Intrinsic (Personal): The mental faculty that translates experience into countable elements so ratios and trends can be perceived.

Extrinsic (Interpersonal): The pattern recognition that allows groups to compare effort and assess progress without relying solely on perception.

Integrative (Systemic): The principle that number provides structural insight, enabling systems to learn from accumulation rather than from anecdote.

The ARAA Sequence:

Awareness - When to Use This Symbol

Identify the environmental cues that signal a lack of measurable clarity:

- Decisions are being made based on feelings or impressions rather than on measurement.
- The actual scale of a problem or a project is being underestimated or exaggerated.
- Progress is discussed in abstract terms but is not being actively tracked or recorded.
- Patterns in behavior or results are suspected but remain unverified by data.

Awareness - When to Use This Symbol (continued)

- The effort expended and the final outcome feel disconnected or disproportionate.

Reflection - Diagnostic Questions

Assess the quantitative reality of your current situation:

- What specific elements of this situation can be counted or measured right now?

- What patterns emerge when this specific quantity is tracked over a period of time?

- Where might my intuition be misleading me because I lack actual data?

- What does the repetition of this specific process reveal about its effectiveness?

Analysis - Failure Modes

Analyze the potential for the distortion of measurement:

Overuse (Reductionism): Treating the number as the entire meaning of the work; measuring only what is easy to count rather than what matters.

Underuse (Generalization): Grounding your life in vague impressions; ignoring numerical patterns that would reveal your actual failures.

Action - Use It Now

Manifest the insight through disciplined behavior:

Choose one ongoing activity and track a single relevant quantity over time; observe what pattern becomes visible from the data.

Geometry

The System for Organizing Relationship and Form

Geometry governs the relationships of space and proportion, translating number into form to reveal how parts relate within a whole. It provides the conceptual bridge between abstract principles and lived reality, organizing the world through spatial relation and design.

The Lenses

Intrinsic (Personal): The mental faculty that perceives structure and coherence beyond isolated measurements or individual parts.

Extrinsic (Interpersonal): The spatial relation that allows individuals and elements to be positioned appropriately to prevent collision or isolation.

Integrative (Systemic): The principle that structure reveals truth; systems endure when their form reflects the relationships they are meant to sustain.

The ARAA Sequence:

Awareness - When to Use This Symbol

Identify the environmental cues that signal a lack of structural coherence:

- Individual parts or efforts exist within a project but do not actually integrate.
- Growth is occurring, but it is creating complexity without any corresponding coherence.
- Your current structures, professional or personal, feel unstable despite your effort.
- Relationships or projects are competing for the same limited space or attention.

Awareness - When to Use This Symbol (continued)

- Expansion is being pursued without any underlying design or plan for integration.

Reflection - Diagnostic Questions

Assess the proportion and relationship of the elements you are working with:

- What specific form is actually emerging from these disparate elements?

- Are the current relationships between these parts proportionate and coherent?

- Where does the underlying structure need refinement before any further growth?

- What happens to this system if the scale changes will the current form hold?

Analysis - Failure Modes

Analyze the potential for the distortion of form:

Overuse (Over-Engineering): Obsessing over structure to the point of stifling function; creating beautiful but rigid architectures that cannot adapt.

Underuse (Fragmentation): Expanding without a design; accumulating parts without a plan, resulting in a work that collapses under its own weight.

Action - Use It Now

Manifest the insight through disciplined behavior:

Take a project or system that feels unwieldy and sketch its parts and relationships; adjust the proportion until coherence emerges.

Music

The System for Ordering Experience through Patterned Time

Music governs patterned sound through rhythm, melody, and harmony, organizing time into structured sequences that can be perceived and shared. It makes the patterns of life audible, coordinating movement, emotion, and attention across individuals by ordering experience through cadence rather than force.

The Lenses

Intrinsic (Personal): The mental faculty that perceives internal rhythm, emotional cadence, and coherence across the unfolding experiences of one's life.

Extrinsic (Interpersonal): The emotional resonance that aligns attention and feeling, allowing groups to coordinate through attunement without explicit instruction.

Integrative (Systemic): The principle that systems express their health through rhythm, where stability and vitality depend on how energy moves through a structure over time.

The ARAA Sequence:

Awareness - When to Use This Symbol

Identify the environmental cues that signal a failure of rhythm or resonance:

- Sustained effort feels exhausting or jarring despite having a sound logical structure.
- Communication with others feels flat, mis-timed, or emotionally discordant.
- A group or team struggles to move together in sync toward a common goal.
- The pace of work alternates erratically between stagnation and frantic urgency.

Awareness - When to Use This Symbol (continued)

- The emotional tone of an interaction is actively undermining your stated intentions.

Reflection - Diagnostic Questions

Assess the cadence and tone of your current interactions:

- What specific rhythm is currently governing this process or interaction?

- Where is the cadence of my work or speech too fast, too slow, or uneven?

- What emotional tone am I expressing unintentionally through my timing?

- How might adjusting the rhythm of this situation restore its overall coherence?

Analysis - Failure Modes

Analyze the potential for the distortion of pattern and tempo:

Overuse (The Forced Tempo): Forcing a specific rhythm or volume onto a situation without regard for others; mistaking intensity for effectiveness until the system shatters from the vibration of force.

Underuse (The Flat Life): Treating emotion and rhythm as noise to be ignored in favor of pure utility; ignoring signs of depletion until burnout occurs.

Action - Use It Now

Manifest the insight through disciplined behavior:

Observe one ongoing activity; notice its rhythm, the pace, the pauses, and the flow, and adjust the timing to improve its sustainability and resonance.

Astronomy

The System for Orientation within Scale and Context

Astronomy governs the observation of celestial bodies to reveal regular cycles and relative positions. It enables navigation and orientation by situating local activity within larger patterns and systems that exceed immediate perception.

The Lenses

Intrinsic (Personal): The mental faculty that contextualizes experience, placing events and decisions within broader patterns of time and scale.

Extrinsic (Interpersonal): The recognition of interconnected scale, where individual actions are understood as part of larger systems, cycles, and histories.

Integrative (Systemic): The principle that order exists across vast scales; systems function best when aligned with larger rhythms rather than resisting them.

The ARAA Sequence:

Awareness – When to Use This Symbol

Identify the environmental cues that signal a collapse of perspective:

- Immediate, local concerns feel overwhelmingly important or catastrophic.
- Decisions are being made without regard for their long-term or systemic consequences.
- Your perspective on a situation collapses entirely under the weight of current urgency.
- Your sense of responsibility is either vastly inflated or completely abdicated.
- Essential context is being lost because you are buried in the minute details.

Reflection - Diagnostic Questions

Assess the scale and context of your current situation:

- What larger system or cycle is this specific event actually a part of?
- How does changing the scale of my perspective change the significance of this issue?
- What long-term timing or natural rhythm am I currently ignoring in my haste?
- Where would a dose of humility restore my clarity rather than diminish my agency?

Analysis - Failure Modes

Analyze the potential for the distortion of scope:

Overuse (Abstraction): Using the vastness of scale to evade local responsibility; romanticizing insignificance to avoid the friction of the Work.

Underuse (Myopia): Collapsing your entire reality into the current moment; ignoring rhythms of interdependence, leading to a life driven by constant crisis.

Action - Use It Now

Manifest the insight through disciplined behavior:

When urgency dominates your judgment, expand the frame; place the situation within a larger temporal or systemic context and reassess your response.

The Craft

The System for Coordinated Labor

The Craft is the shared operating language through which individuals align effort, divide responsibility, and produce outcomes no one person could achieve alone. It is the mode through which skill, trust, and accountability are translated into coordinated, collective action.

The Lenses

Intrinsic (Personal): The competency of individual participation, where the Mason learns to work in sequence and dependency with others.

Extrinsic (Interpersonal): The dynamic of mutual interdependence, where progress emerges from reciprocal responsibility and shared trust.

Integrative (Systemic): The principle of collective fluency; the ability of a system to maintain standards and continuity that outlast individual involvement.

The ARAA Sequence:

Awareness - When to Use This Symbol

Identify the environmental cues that signal a failure of coordination:

- Your work feels siloed or isolated despite having shared goals with others.
- High individual effort is being expended but is not translating into collective progress.
- Formal roles exist in the group, but the coordination between those roles is faltering.
- Communication breakdowns are creating recurring friction, delay, or wasted effort.

Awareness - When to Use This Symbol (continued)

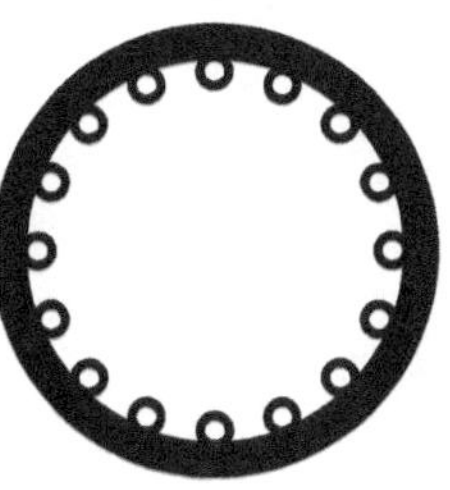

- Accountability is being treated as a personal burden rather than a shared standard.

Reflection - Diagnostic Questions

Assess the fluency of your participation in the system:

- How fluent am I actually in the shared working language of this specific group?

- Where exactly is the coordination breaking down, and what is the likely cause?

- How do my specific actions enable or impede the ability of others to do their work?

- What standards or expectations need to be reinforced to improve our collective flow?

Analysis - Failure Modes

Analyze the potential for the distortion of collective work:

Overuse (Collective Erasure): Hiding behind a group identity to avoid individual responsibility; treating the system as an audience for your belonging rather than a structure for your contribution.

Underuse (Isolationism): Prioritizing individual heroic effort over coordinated success; ignoring dependencies until the entire system fractures.

Action - Use It Now

Manifest the insight through disciplined behavior:

Identify one ongoing effort involving multiple people; observe how work is coordinated and adjust one behavior—timing or follow-through—to improve fluency.

Elements

Elements describe the structural principles underlying effective design. These symbols such as the orders of architecture or the pillars of the porch provide the criteria for evaluating whether a life or a project is fit for purpose, stable, and elegant in its construction.

Boaz

The Element of Disciplined Strength

Boaz is represented as the left-hand pillar on the porch of the Temple, signifying strength, the capacity to endure weight and resist collapse under pressure. It provides the sustaining force necessary for any structure to hold firm without becoming rigid or aggressive.

The Lenses

Intrinsic (Personal): The mental faculty that holds firm under strain without becoming rigid, allowing for fortitude and resilience in the face of adversity.

Extrinsic (Interpersonal): The stabilizing force of a consistent presence that allows others to rely on and coordinate with you without fear of failure.

Integrative (Systemic): The principle that power is the structural capacity to bear load, ensuring that strength precedes expansion in any healthy system.

The ARAA Sequence:

Awareness - When to Use This Symbol

Identify the environmental cues that signal a failure of strength or resilience:

- Current responsibilities have begun to outpace your internal resilience or capacity.
- External pressure is exposing hidden structural weaknesses in your character or plans.
- Authority is being claimed or asserted without the actual capacity to back it up.
- Systems or projects are beginning to strain and wobble under the weight of growth.

Awareness - When to Use This Symbol (continued)

- Disciplined endurance is being confused with or replaced by outward aggression.

Reflection - Diagnostic Questions

Assess your current capacity to bear the weight of your obligations:

- What specific load or responsibility am I actually being asked to bear right now?

- Where does my internal strength need to increase before I attempt further expansion?

- Am I truly holding firm to my principles, or am I merely resisting necessary change?

- What would disciplined, quiet endurance look like in this specific situation?

Analysis - Failure Modes

Analyze the potential for the distortion of power:

Overuse (Stasis): Mistaking strength for a refusal to move; you become a roadblock, resisting even the changes required to improve the structure.

Underuse (Fragility): Collapsing at the first sign of friction; you rely on others for stability, making you a burden rather than a pillar.

Action - Use It Now

Manifest the insight through disciplined behavior:

Identify a responsibility that feels heavy; assess whether your current strength is sufficient, and reinforce your capacity before increasing the demand.

Jachin

The Element of Firm Establishment

Jachin is the right-hand pillar on the porch of the Temple, signifying establishment; the act of setting conditions so that strength can function reliably. It represents the fixing of reference points, principles, and shared expectations so that action can proceed without constant renegotiation.

The Lenses

Intrinsic (Personal): The mental faculty that fixes internal reference points, principles and commitments, to enable steady action.

Extrinsic (Interpersonal): The setting of shared expectations and standards so that others can orient their behavior with confidence and clarity.

Integrative (Systemic): The principle that systems require firm establishment to function coherently, embedding purpose into the very structure of the work.

The ARAA Sequence:

Awareness - When to Use This Symbol

Identify the environmental cues that signal a lack of firm foundation:

- Effort is high and strength is present, but the overall direction remains unclear.
- Roles, rules, or standards of conduct shift unpredictably from day to day.
- Systems are relying on constant course correction rather than proper initial setup.
- Rework and correction are consuming more energy than actual forward progress.

Awareness - When to Use This Symbol (continued)

- Stability depends entirely on individual force or personality rather than on structure.

Reflection - Diagnostic Questions

Assess the foundations of your current project or role:

- What specific foundation or rule has not been properly established in this situation?

- Where do expectations need to be explicitly set to prevent future confusion?

- What foundation would prevent the need for repeated correction or intervention later?

- How can my purpose be embedded structurally rather than through constant enforcement?

Analysis - Failure Modes

Analyze the potential for the distortion of establishment:

Overuse (Orthodoxy): Obsessing over rules and alignment to the point of stifling life; mistaking the uprightness of the pillar for the entirety of the building.

Underuse (Drift): Failing to establish clear standards; allowing your life to lean into convenience, leading to a collapse that raw strength cannot prevent.

Action - Use It Now

Manifest the insight through disciplined behavior:

Before applying further effort or authority, establish the foundation, clarify expectations, set reference points, and fix what must remain stable.

Tuscan

The Element of Robust Simplicity

Tuscan represents the earliest and simplest of the classical architectural orders, emphasizing stability and utility over expression. It is defined by plain form and minimal ornamentation, establishing the workable foundation required for first principles to take root without confusion.

The Lenses

Intrinsic (Personal): The mental faculty that strips complexity down to essentials so that work can begin clearly and without distraction.

Extrinsic (Interpersonal): The establishment of fundamental clarity through simple structures, reducing misunderstanding and enabling cooperation.

Integrative (Systemic): The principle that systems endure when built from first principles; function must always precede expression.

The ARAA Sequence:

Awareness - When to Use This Symbol

Identify the environmental cues that signal over-complication:

- The systems you are working within feel fragile, unanchored, or over-engineered.
- High levels of complexity are appearing before basic functionality has been achieved.
- Essential work is stalling because of excessive planning or feature creep.
- Reliability is being sacrificed in favor of perceived sophistication or status.
- The foundational assumptions of a project or relationship are fundamentally unclear.

Reflection - Diagnostic Questions

Assess the essentials of your current design:

- What is actually essential for this specific thing to function as intended?

- What can be removed right now without any loss of the primary purpose?

- Where has unnecessary complexity replaced the need for fundamental clarity?

- What first principle have I overlooked or ignored in my current approach?

Analysis - Failure Modes

Analyze the potential for the distortion of simplicity:

Overuse (Brutality): Using simplicity as an excuse for being crude or thoughtless; damaging delicate people or subtle projects through lack of refinement.

Underuse (Fragility): Attempting to be sophisticated before you are stable; adding ornament to a life that lacks the unadorned strength to hold it up.

Action - Use It Now

Manifest the insight through disciplined behavior:

Take a project or system that feels fragile; strip it back to its essentials and rebuild only what is required for reliable function.

Doric

The Element of Visible Strength

Doric is characterized by robust proportions and fluted columns, expressing strength and stability through form rather than ornament. It conveys a seriousness of purpose, structuring power so that it can be expressed steadily and predictably over time.

The Lenses

Intrinsic (Personal): The mental faculty that organizes internal effort so that power is expressed through disciplined form rather than explosive impulse.

Extrinsic (Interpersonal): The removal of unnecessary relational complexity to preserve strength and ensure straightforward expectations.

Integrative (Systemic): The principle that stability emerges from essential form; proportion preserves integrity where added ornament undermines it.

The ARAA Sequence:

Awareness - When to Use This Symbol

Identify the environmental cues that signal a failure of disciplined form:

- Your systems or habits are failing despite high levels of sustained demand.
- You are expending significant effort, but your actual resilience remains low.
- Strength is being asserted through words or posture rather than being embodied in action.
- Your structures rely on constant force rather than on their underlying form.

Awareness - When to Use This Symbol (continued)

- Long-term durability has been sacrificed in favor of immediate speed or convenience.

Reflection - Diagnostic Questions

Assess the reinforcement of your current structures:

- Where does the underlying structure of this situation need more reinforcement?

- What specific load must this current form be able to reliably bear?

- Where has excess complexity or noise weakened my actual strength?

- What specific discipline or habit would best stabilize this current system?

Analysis - Failure Modes

Analyze the potential for the distortion of discipline:

Overuse (Rigidity): Becoming so obsessed with the rules of your life that you lose the ability to adapt; becoming a stone statue that cannot move.

Underuse (Sloppiness): Relying on raw talent or effort while refusing the labor of discipline; resulting in work that is unreliable under sustained pressure.

Action - Use It Now

Manifest the insight through disciplined behavior:

Identify an area where fatigue or failure is recurring; reinforce the underlying structure through repetition or discipline before increasing the demand.

Ionic

The Element of Refined Adaptability

Ionic introduces articulation and elegance through slender proportions and characteristic volutes. It represents the maturation of form, refining expression to improve fit and responsiveness without undermining the structural foundation.

The Lenses

Intrinsic (Personal): The mental faculty that adjusts behavior and language to fit the context without weakening the underlying foundation.

Extrinsic (Interpersonal): The harmonization of nuance that integrates different perspectives smoothly, reducing friction without erasing distinction.

Integrative (Systemic): The principle that systems mature through refinement rather than replacement, increasing adaptability through iterative improvement.

The ARAA Sequence:

Awareness - When to Use This Symbol

Identify the environmental cues that signal a lack of refinement:

- Your structures are stable but feel coarse, inflexible, or out of place.
- Your outward expression lags behind your actual internal capability or skill.
- Constructive feedback is available to you but has not yet been integrated into your work.
- Adaptation to a new situation is needed, but you fear losing your core strength.
- A system feels functional but is increasingly misaligned with its current context.

Reflection - Diagnostic Questions

Assess the fit of your current approach:

- What specific element can be refined here without weakening the core structure?

- Where would a bit of nuance improve the fit or the clarity of this interaction?

- What specific feedback have I received that I have not yet integrated into my process?

- How can my expression evolve here while still preserving my foundational strength?

Analysis - Failure Modes

Analyze the potential for the distortion of nuance:

Overuse (Indecision): Becoming so enamored with nuance that you fail to provide actual support; your scrolls obscure your column, leading to moral ambiguity.

Underuse (Callousness): Refusing to adapt your style to the person or the moment; appearing robotic, which causes relational mortar to crumble.

Action - Use It Now

Manifest the insight through disciplined behavior:

Take a stable system or habit; make one small, intentional refinement that improves its fit or clarity without altering its core structure.

Corinthian

The Element of Aesthetic Excellence

Corinthian is distinguished by elaborate ornamentation and slender proportions, elevating presence through decorative detail. It represents the enrichment of form, adding beauty and flourish to inspire and uplift once structure and refinement are secure.

The Lenses

Intrinsic (Personal): The mental faculty that invests effort in elegance, care, and detail once the foundational work is stable.

Extrinsic (Interpersonal): The uplift of relational presence through thoughtful detail, signaling respect and appreciation to others.

Integrative (Systemic): The principle that beauty signals flourishing; aesthetic care reinforces meaning and pride within a stable system.

The ARAA Sequence:

Awareness - When to Use This Symbol

Identify the environmental cues that signal a lack of inspiration:

- A system or relationship functions well but feels uninspiring or gray.
- Care and attention to detail have been deprioritized in favor of pure utility.
- Your environments or interactions feel purely transactional and lacking in warmth.
- Meaning is technically present in the work, but it is not being felt by anyone.
- Your expression or environment lacks a sense of generosity or finishing polish.

Reflection - Diagnostic Questions

Assess the enrichment of your current work:

- Where would a bit of enrichment elevate the experience without weakening the structure?

- What specific details would communicate a sense of care and significance here?

- Has ornament been delayed too long in this project or was it introduced too early?

- How can I use beauty to reinforce the actual meaning of what I am doing?

Analysis - Failure Modes

Analyze the potential for the distortion of beauty:

Overuse (Baroque Excess): Becoming so lost in the leaves of decoration that you forget your purpose; valuing style over substance in a hollow structure.

Underuse (The Unfinished Work): Stopping at good enough when excellence is required; depriving yourself of the inspiration that comes from a fully realized effort.

Action - Use It Now

Manifest the insight through disciplined behavior:

Identify a stable, refined relationship or system; add one intentional element of beauty or care that enriches the experience without altering function.

Composite

The Element of Unifying Synthesis

Composite integrates features of the prior orders, specifically Ionic and Corinthian, into a single, coherent form. Its function is the unification of established, mature principles into a stable whole that reflects consolidation after growth.

The Lenses

Intrinsic (Personal): The mental faculty that reconciles strength, refinement, and beauty into a single, coherent expression.

Extrinsic (Interpersonal): The synthesis across parts where distinct roles or perspectives are brought together without erasing their unique identities.

Integrative (Systemic): The principle that maturity expresses itself through unification; durability is reached when all mature forms are harmonized.

The ARAA Sequence:

Awareness - When to Use This Symbol

Identify the environmental cues that signal a lack of integration:

- Multiple different strengths exist in your life but remain siloed or disconnected.
- A system feels technically complete but remains fragmented in its actual operation.
- The integration of your various skills or roles is lagging behind your actual development.
- Complexity is accumulating in your life without a corresponding sense of coherence.
- You are seeking innovation when what you actually need is a synthesis of what works.

Reflection - Diagnostic Questions

Assess the harmony of your mature elements:

- What specific elements of my life or work are now mature enough to be integrated?

- Where does a combination of elements improve coherence rather than just adding complexity?

- What proven, stable forms should I preserve and unify rather than replace?

- How can unity emerge in this situation without flattening the distinctions of the parts?

Analysis - Failure Modes

Analyze the potential for the distortion of synthesis:

Overuse (Eclecticism): Combining elements haphazardly without a unifying logic; mistaking messy complexity for genuine synthesis.

Underuse (Purity Trap): Refusing to adapt or blend your approach; failing to solve a problem because your toolkit is dogmatically narrow.

Action - Use It Now

Manifest the insight through disciplined behavior:

Identify a mature system with multiple functioning parts; integrate two complementary elements into a unified whole while preserving their unique strengths.

Foundations

Foundations describe the enduring truths and cosmic patterns that shape human experience. These symbols articulate the fundamental realities; labor and rest, duality and unity, cause and consequence, within which all work is conducted. They orient the Mason toward the unchanging principles governing existence.

Sun

The Foundation of Conscious Illumination

The Sun governs the cycle of visibility and labor, providing the light and warmth necessary for growth and activity. It represents the faculty of clarity, enabling the Mason to make distinctions, clarify perceptions, and direct energy toward purposeful effort when conditions are visible.

The Lenses

Intrinsic (Personal): The mental faculty that clarifies perception and enables deliberate effort by making distinctions visible within the mind.

Extrinsic (Interpersonal): The act of bringing clarity into relationships, reducing ambiguity and surfacing expectations to foster shared accountability.

Integrative (Systemic): The principle that transformation requires illumination; systems evolve only when structures and consequences are made fully visible.

The ARAA Sequence:

Awareness - When to Use This Symbol

Identify when work is proceeding in the dark:

- Action is proceeding despite a lack of clear understanding or a defined plan.
- Ambiguity regarding roles or expectations is obscuring individual responsibility.
- Effort feels misdirected, premature, or based on guesswork rather than facts.
- Foundational assumptions are persisting unexamined because they haven't been brought to light.
- Accountability feels diffuse or impossible because the outcomes are not being tracked.

Reflection - Diagnostic Questions

Assess the level of light currently shining on your work:

- What specific aspect of this situation needs to be brought into the light right now?

- Where exactly is clarity required before I allow this action to continue?

- What distinctions or definitions are currently blurred in my perception?

- How would increasing visibility and illumination improve our collective coordination?

Analysis - Failure Modes

Analyze the distortion of illumination:

Overuse (The Scorcher): Demanding absolute, blinding transparency at all times; burning out others by exposing every detail to scrutiny before it is ready.

Underuse (The Sleeper): Operating in a state of denial; avoiding hard facts to keep errors hidden from yourself and the world.

Action - Use It Now

Manifest the insight through disciplined behavior:

Identify one area where effort feels misaligned; explicitly surface the facts and assumptions, and act only once visibility has improved.

Moon

The Foundation of Restorative Pacing

The Moon governs the rhythms of the night, influencing tides and biological cycles to regulate the alternation between activity and recovery. It represents the faculty of restorative pacing, creating the necessary conditions for integration, reflection, and emotional replenishment.

The Lenses

Intrinsic (Personal): The mental faculty that allows for withdrawal, reflection, and emotional processing without it becoming avoidance.

Extrinsic (Interpersonal): The management of relational pacing, recognizing that connections require cycles of engagement and rest to remain healthy.

Integrative (Systemic): The principle that renewal is a structural law of development; systems that do not pause for recovery will eventually degrade.

The ARAA Sequence:

Awareness - When to Use This Symbol

Identify when the cycle of renewal has been broken:

- Accumulated fatigue is starting to undermine your judgment and clarity.
- Emotional reactivity is increasing because you lack the space to process experiences.
- Effort is persisting despite clearly diminishing returns on your investment of energy.
- Burnout is being disguised or marketed as a form of high-performance discipline.
- Necessary reflection is being postponed indefinitely in favor of more doing.

Reflection - Diagnostic Questions

Assess your current need for recovery and integration:

- What specific part of my life or work needs to rest before it can function again?

- Where has my recent exertion exceeded my actual capacity for recovery?

- What emotional residue or unprocessed experience requires my attention right now?

- How can I restore a natural pacing to my work without fully withdrawing from my duties?

Analysis - Failure Modes

Analyze the distortion of restorative cycles:

Overuse (The Lunatic): Being governed entirely by shifting moods and internal tides; mistaking subjective feelings for objective reality.

Underuse (The Robotic): Having no capacity for self-correction; driving forward with objective data while ignoring the subtle intuitive signals of the night.

Action - Use It Now

Manifest the insight through disciplined behavior:

Identify one area of sustained effort and pause deliberately; allow for rest and integration before you continue with the task.

The Pavement

The Foundation of Discernment within Contrast

The Pavement is a checkered surface of alternating light and dark, representing the mixed conditions of human existence. It serves as a foundation for movement across opposites, enabling the Mason to recognize contrast and duality without collapsing into fragmentation or choosing sides.

The Lenses

Intrinsic (Personal): The mental faculty that recognizes opposition and contrast within the self without seeking to eliminate the tension.

Extrinsic (Interpersonal): The steady engagement with difference, allowing connections to persist through disagreement and asymmetry.

Integrative (Systemic): The principle of the non-dual ground, acknowledging that contrast is intrinsic to manifestation and stability comes from the surface beneath the pattern.

The ARAA Sequence:

Awareness - When to Use This Symbol

Identify when reality is being flattened into a false binary:

- Situations are being framed as either/or choices when both elements are present.
- Moral certainty or purity is being used to bypass the need for practical wisdom.
- Conflict is escalating because parties are polarizing into opposing black and white camps.
- Ambiguity or the presence of a shadow is being treated as a sign of failure.

- One side of a situation is being idealized while the other is being totally rejected.

Reflection - Diagnostic Questions

Assess the ground on which you are standing:

- What specific opposites or contrasts are being falsely separated in this situation?

- Where am I insisting on a pure outcome rather than accepting the truth of the mix?

- What remains constant and stable beneath the shifting patterns of this contrast?

- How can I proceed with the work without demanding an immediate resolution of the tension?

Analysis - Failure Modes

Analyze the potential for the distortion of duality:

Overuse (The Manichaean): Becoming obsessed with binary choices (good/evil, right/wrong); losing the ability to navigate the gray transitions of real life.

Underuse (The Indiscriminate): Refusing to acknowledge duality; treating light and shadow as the same and failing to distinguish between productive and destructive forces.

Action - Use It Now

Manifest the insight through disciplined behavior:

When faced with a polarized situation, identify the shared ground beneath the opposing positions and choose an action without demanding a winner.

As Above, So Below

The Foundation of Reflective Correspondence

As Above, So Below expresses the principle of correspondence, where patterns repeat across different scales of reality. It reveals the relationship between the macro and the micro, affirming that internal posture mirrors external action and that small compromises can scale into systemic failures.

The Lenses

Intrinsic (Personal): The mental faculty that aligns inner intention and thought with outer conduct and impact.

Extrinsic (Interpersonal): The recognition of reflective dynamics, where the patterns present in one domain of a relationship tend to reappear in others.

Integrative (Systemic): The principle of unity of pattern across scales, ensuring that micro-behaviors consistently reflect macro-values.

The ARAA Sequence:

Awareness - When to Use This Symbol

Identify the echoes across different scales of your work:

- The same outcomes or frustrations are recurring across entirely different contexts.
- Core values are being professed at a high level but are not being enacted in daily tasks.
- Your inner intention for a situation is in direct conflict with your actual external impact.
- Small, minor compromises are beginning to scale into large, systemic problems.
- Your daily behavior feels disconnected from your overall sense of purpose or vision.

Reflection - Diagnostic Questions

Assess the correspondence between your levels of engagement:

- Where specifically does my inner posture show up in my outer, visible life?

- What specific small pattern in this moment mirrors a larger pattern in my history?

- Where exactly is the alignment breaking down between my vision and my execution?

- What adjustment at the smallest possible scale would correct the larger systemic pattern?

Analysis - Failure Modes

Analyze the potential for the distortion of correspondence:

Overuse (The Escapist Architect): Theorizing about the grand ideal while your actual life falls into ruin; using higher purpose to ignore mundane labor.

Underuse (The Myopic Laborer): Focusing so intensely on technical details that you lose all connection to the purpose of the work; building a wall while forgetting the Temple.

Action - Use It Now

Manifest the insight through disciplined behavior:

Identify a recurring issue across different domains; adjust the smallest controllable pattern and observe how the larger system responds.

Grand Architect of the Universe (GAOTU)

The Foundation of Transcendent Orientation

GAOTU represents the highest principle of order and intelligibility, serving as a supreme point of reference that precedes personal opinion. It is not a creed but a unifying orientation that allows diverse workmen to submit their actions to a principle higher than their own preferences.

The Lenses

Intrinsic (Personal): The mental faculty that recognizes the limits of personal perspective and submits action to a principle higher than impulse or appetite.

Extrinsic (Interpersonal): The shared grounding that enables cooperation across differences of belief by referring to a common axis of purpose.

Integrative (Systemic): The principle of transcendent order, providing the orienting architecture that prevents a system from collapsing into power struggles.

The ARAA Sequence:

Awareness - When to Use This Symbol

Identify when the work has lost its highest reference:

- Decisions are defaulting to personal preference, convenience, or expedience.
- Authority in the group or in yourself is becoming personalized, arbitrary, or ego-driven.
- Shared meaning is eroding because members are focused on their individual identities.
- Intellectual or moral humility is giving way to a dangerous sense of certainty.
- The system is losing its orientation toward anything beyond its own survival or process.

Reflection - Diagnostic Questions

Assess your submission to the laws of the architecture:

- What is the highest possible principle that should govern this specific decision?

- Where am I currently substituting my own preference for a legitimate reference point?

- What specific orientation would allow for cooperation here despite our differences?

- What does true humility, not self-diminishment, require of me in this moment?

Analysis - Failure Modes

Analyze the potential for the distortion of ultimate reference:

Overuse (The Fatalist/Pre-Determiner): Using The Design to bypass your own agency; assuming that if there is a plan, your effort doesn't matter.

Underuse (The Hubristic/Chaos-Maker): Acting as the only designer; believing you can force the stone to behave however you want without regard for systemic laws.

Action - Use It Now

Manifest the insight through disciplined behavior:

Before acting under uncertainty, explicitly name the principle you are referring to and adjust your action to align with it rather than with pressure.

Milestones

Milestones describe the movement from potential to refinement. These symbols mark the stages of a man's labor and the ultimate aim of his life. They serve as a map for the path from the rough ashlar of raw potential to the temple of a coherent, meaningful life.

Rough Ashlar

The Milestone of Honest Raw Condition

The Rough Ashlar represents the unworked or imperfect stone as it comes from the quarry, acknowledging the reality of imperfection and unrefined potential. It serves as a reminder that development must begin with an honest assessment of the rough edges, the habits and distortions, that are not yet fit for integration into a larger structure.

The Lenses

Intrinsic (Personal): The mental faculty that identifies internal distortions, habits, and excesses without the interference of denial or self-condemnation.

Extrinsic (Interpersonal): The interaction with others that exposes irregularities, such as defensiveness or immaturity, that remain hidden in isolation.

Integrative (Systemic): The principle that development begins through negation; identifying what does not belong and cutting it away before building occurs.

The ARAA Sequence:

Awareness - When to Use This Symbol

Identify when growth is being obstructed by unacknowledged flaws:

- You desire personal or professional growth but refuse to acknowledge your current limitations.
- High ideals or aspirations are being used to replace an honest assessment of your current state.
- Repeated friction in your life or relationships signals a specific, unaddressed roughness.
- External feedback is being avoided or dismissed because it challenges your self-image.

Awareness - When to Use This Symbol (continued)

- You are attempting advanced refinement or leadership before your foundations are squared.

Reflection - Diagnostic Questions

Assess the material you are actually working with right now:

- What specific irregularities or flaws in my character must be addressed first?

- Where am I currently pretending to be finished or perfect to avoid the work?

- What specific developmental effort have I been actively avoiding out of fear or pride?

- What specific part of my nature must be removed before a clear form can emerge?

Analysis - Failure Modes

Analyze the potential for the distortion of raw potential:

Overuse (The Fetishist of Authenticity): Mistaking your unrefined impulses and flaws for being real; refusing refinement because you believe discipline is a betrayal of your true self.

Underuse (The Perfectionist Pretender): Being so ashamed of your rough state that you hide it under social performance; refusing to acknowledge the material you actually have to work with.

Action - Use It Now

Manifest the insight through disciplined behavior:

Identify one persistent friction, internal or external; name it plainly, and begin removing what clearly does not serve, without demanding immediate perfection.

Perfect Ashlar

The Milestone of Reliable Integration

The Perfect Ashlar represents a stone that has been worked, squared, and polished until it is fit for its intended place in the structure. It signifies the achievement of coherence, habits, conduct, and intention aligned through effort, marking the point where an individual becomes reliable enough to be counted on without constant adjustment.

The Lenses

Intrinsic (Personal): The mental faculty that achieves internal coherence, aligning form and function so behavior is consistent and dependable.

Extrinsic (Interpersonal): The establishment of trust through consistency witnessed by others, where reliability allows for collaboration without constant vigilance.

Integrative (Systemic): The principle that coherence is the measure of maturity; parts are fit for placement within a larger architecture only when they function predictably.

The ARAA Sequence:

Awareness - When to Use This Symbol

Identify when improvement lacks the stability of integration:

- Significant improvement has occurred in your life, but it has not yet been integrated into a stable habit.

- You possess individual strengths, but they lack the dependability required for high-stakes work.

- Your personal growth feels episodic or burst-oriented rather than stable and predictable.

- Your participation in a group still requires constant monitoring or checking in by others.

Awareness - When to Use This Symbol (continued)

- Your outward form and your inward function remain misaligned despite your best efforts.

Reflection - Diagnostic Questions

Assess the reliability of your current character:

- Is my behavior in this specific area reliable under normal conditions and pressures?

- Where exactly does inconsistency still appear in my daily conduct or speech?

- What specific part of my internal integration remains incomplete or wobbly?

- Is my current refinement truly structural or is it merely a cosmetic social performance?

Analysis - Failure Modes

Analyze the potential for the distortion of completion:

Overuse (The Finished Statue): Believing you have reached perfection and are exempt from further growth; becoming a brittle monument to past achievements.

Underuse (The Functional Failure): Stopping refinement at good enough; settling for being a smoothish stone that still possesses hidden slants that crack under pressure.

Action - Use It Now

Manifest the insight through disciplined behavior:

Review a habit, role, or responsibility; assess its reliability and complete one final adjustment to improve consistency before you take on additional load.

The Temple

The Milestone of Collective Realization

The Temple represents the completed structure formed from many properly prepared and integrated stones, assembled according to a shared design. It signifies the transition from individual excellence to collective integration, where meaning arises from placing one's refined work in service of a purpose larger and more enduring than the self.

The Lenses

Intrinsic (Personal): The mental faculty that recognizes when individual effort has matured into participation in something lasting and transcendent.

Extrinsic (Interpersonal): The coordination of shared purpose where individual differences are subordinated to a collective design.

Integrative (Systemic): The principle that enduring structures arise from disciplined integration over time; the visible consequence of invisible discipline.

The ARAA Sequence:

Awareness - When to Use This Symbol

Identify when effort lacks collective impact or continuity:

- Your hard work feels isolated, inconsequential, or disconnected from any larger meaning.
- Individual excellence in a group is failing to produce any tangible collective impact.
- Your current work lacks continuity or a sense of being built to last across generations.
- Your primary purpose remains abstract or aspirational rather than being embodied in a structure.

Awareness - When to Use This Symbol (continued)

- Your contribution to a project is seeking individual recognition rather than proper placement.

Reflection - Diagnostic Questions

Assess the placement of your contribution within the whole:

- What specific larger structure or design does my current work actually serve?

- Where exactly does my personal contribution need more refinement before it is fit for placement?

- Am I currently focused on building a shared structure or am I merely expressing myself?

- What specific design or blueprint governs our collective effort in this moment?

Analysis - Failure Modes

Analyze the potential for the distortion of the grand design:

Overuse (The Utopian Architect): Obsessing over the Grand Idea while ignoring the reality of the individual stones; sacrificing quality for the sake of the Finished Image.

Underuse (The Disconnected Laborer): Focusing entirely on your own stone with no regard for the blueprints; producing a Perfect Ashlar that doesn't fit the wall.

Action - Use It Now

Manifest the insight through disciplined behavior:

Consider a contribution you are making to a group; align it explicitly to the shared design and place it there without attachment to personal recognition.

Conclusion

Freemasonry has long been described as a progressive science, yet for generations, that progress has been measured by the steady accumulation of ritual memory rather than the tangible transformation of the man. We have inherited a magnificent architecture of symbols, but we have lived in it as tenants rather than craftsmen, admiring the structure without understanding the tools required to maintain or expand it.

The work presented in these pages is an attempt to move the craft from the museum to the workshop. By reclaiming the Operative identity of our speculative tradition, we acknowledge that the lodge is not merely a social destination, but a developmental necessity. In an era defined by the collapse of traditional social scaffolding and the rise of algorithmic noise, the lodge offers a rare and vital alternative: a secular pastoral infrastructure where a man is neither a consumer nor a data point, but a workman at his own stone.

The *Operative Protocol*, moving from the orientation of the Space to the authority of the Role and the constraint of the Tool, is the mechanism for this recovery. It provides the mental handrails necessary to translate the ritual's high ideals into the grit of daily conduct. When we use the Secretary to audit our patterns, the Junior Warden to regulate our vitality, or the Square to validate our actions, we are no longer practicing a hobby; we are engaged in the intentional refinement of consciousness.

However, the word of the craft cannot be found in a book; it must be spoken through a life. The symbols do not work unless the man does. A gauge cannot apportion time if the hand refuses to set the boundary, and a trowel can bind nothing if the heart refuses to offer care. The success of this system is measured only by the engaged freemason; the individual who leaves the lodge more capable, more reliable, and more attuned to the harmony and melody of the Grand Architect of the Universe.

The fraternity stands at a threshold. We can continue as a ceremonial association, preserving the forms of a dead art, or we can embrace the adaptive challenge of the present moment. We can become an institution that reliably produces change agents: men who contribute with integrity to their families, their workplaces, and their communities.

The choice is yours.

Annotated Bibliography

Aristotle. *Nicomachean Ethics.* Foundational for the realization of purpose through habituated virtue.

Bauman, Z. (2000). *Liquid Modernity.* Explains the instability of modern identity formation.

Baumeister, R. F., & Vohs, K. D. (2007). *Self-Regulation and internal signals.* (Handbook of Self-Regulation). Supports the claim that without interoceptive signals, regulation remains external rather than developed.

Bell, C. (1992). *Ritual Theory, Ritual Practice.* Provides the framework for the liminal space of the lodge.

Bronfenbrenner, U. (1979). *The Ecology of Human Development.* Establishes the necessity of nested social scaffolding.

Cacioppo, J., & Patrick, W. (2008). *Loneliness.* Explores the psychological impact of the isolation the lodge must mitigate.

Damon, W. (2008). *The Path to Purpose.* Empirical support for the golden thread of purpose in the human experience.

Duncan, M. C. (1866). *Duncan's Masonic Ritual and Monitor.* A standard reference for the symbolic and procedural architecture of the journey.

Emmons, R. A. (1999). *The Psychology of Ultimate Concerns.* Validates meaning as a central organizing force.

Frankl, V. E. (2006). *Man's Search for Meaning.* The primary referent for meaning as an existential anchor.

Geertz, C. (1973). *The Interpretation of Cultures.* Establishes symbols as condensations of meaning that regulate behavior.

Gregg, M. (2018). *Counterproductive.* Provides the critique of modern productivity culture.

Hartman, R. S. (1967). *The Structure of Value.* The source of Formal Axiology for the three-fold symbolic lens.

Heifetz, R. A. (1994). *Leadership Without Easy Answers.* Distinguishes between technical problems and the adaptive challenge of modern masonry.

Hodapp, C. (2021). *Freemasons for Dummies.* (3rd ed.). Wiley. The definitive modern guide for demystifying the craft's structure and history.

Illouz, E. (2019). *The Labor of Care.* Analyzes the performative consumerism the craft resists.

Kegan, R. (1994). *In Over Our Heads.* The developmental basis for the subject-to-object shift.

Kolb, D. A. (1984). *Experiential Learning.* Supports the Awareness-Reflection-Analysis-Action (ARAA) cycle.

Lerner, R. (2002). *Concepts and Theories of Human Development.* Discusses the environmental conditions required for maturation.

May, R. (1953). *Man's Search for Himself.* The underpinning of teleological behavior, shaping character through intent.

McAdams, D. P. (2006). *The Redemptive Self.* The basis for narrative identity and life-story formation.

Norman, D. A. (1993). *Things That Make Us Smart.* Explains cognitive offloading through the use of Working Tools.

Posner, M. I., & Rothbart, M. K. (2007). *Research on self-regulatory awareness.* Validates the need for attention to precede intention.

Putnam, R. D. (2000). *Bowling Alone.* Documents the decline of traditional civic scaffolding.

Turner, V. (1969). *The Ritual Process.* Explains how symbols act as mechanisms for structuring attention.

Twenge, J. (2017). *iGen.* Contextualizes the modern developmental crisis of digital immersion.

Vygotsky, L. S. (1978). *Mind in Society.* Supports symbols as external scaffolds for internal awareness.

Wilber, K. (2000). *Integral Psychology.* Provides the levels of complexity and stages of consciousness framework.

Zuboff, S. (2019). *The Age of Surveillance Capitalism.* Diagnoses algorithmic mentorship.

Modern Influences: Echoes of the Craft

Gardner, H. (1983). *Frames of Mind.* Supports the systems for working as multi-modal intelligences.

Goleman, D. (1995). *Emotional Intelligence.* Modern equivalent for the regulation and centering roles.

Harmon, D. (n.d.). *Story Structure 101.* Informs the recursive narrative of the degrees.

Heath, C., & Heath, D. (2017). *The Power of Moments.* Justifies the ritual degree as a defining moment.

Oldenburg, R. (1989). *The Great Good Place.* Validates the lodge as an essential third place.

Schwartz, R. C. (2021). *No Bad Parts.* Informs the psychology of selves (IFS) for role-work.

Stone, H., & Stone, S. (1989). *Embracing Our Selves.* The source for voice dialogue and functional mirroring.

Category Quick Reference:

Spaces

- The Lodge
- The Preparing Room
- The Examining Room
- The World

Roles

- The Freemason
- The Worshipful Master
- The Senior Deacon
- The Senior Warden
- The Junior Deacon
- The Junior Warden
- The Secretary
- The Treasurer
- The Senior Master of Ceremonies
- The Junior Master of Ceremonies
- The Pursuivant
- The Tyler
- The Chaplain
- The Guide

Tools

- 24" Gauge
- Gavel
- Plumb
- Level
- Square
- Trowel
- Compasses
- Hoodwink
- Entered Apprentice
- Fellowcraft
- Master Mason
- Cabletow
- 3 Knocks
- Left Slipper
- Right Slipper
- Money & Valuables
- Mineral & Metallic Substances
- The Ruffians
- The Volume of Sacred Law

Systems of Meaning

- Grammar
- Rhetoric
- Logic
- Arithmetic
- Geometry
- Music
- Astronomy
- The Craft

Elements

- Boaz
- Jachin
- Tuscan
- Doric
- Ionic
- Corinthian
- Composite

Foundations

- Sun
- Moon
- The Pavement
- As Above, So Below
- Grand Architect of the Universe

Milestones

- Rough Ashlar
- Perfect Ashlar
- The Temple

Index